# STYLE STATEMENT

# STYLE ST

Little, Brown and Company

NEW YORK • BOSTON • LONDON

Carrie McCarthy & Danielle LaPorte

# ATEMENT

*Live by your own design*

PHOTOGRAPHS BY GREGORY CROW

Little, Brown and Company

Hachette Book Group USA

237 Park Avenue, New York, NY 10017

Visit our Web site at www.HachetteBookGroupUSA.com

www.carrieanddanielle.com

First Edition: April 2008

ISBN 978-0-316-06716-4

LCCN 2007929947

10 9 8 7 6 5 4 3 2 1

Designed by Empire Design Studio

Printed in China

*for our sisters*

*We are women entrepreneurs.*
*A designer and a writer,*
*an athlete and an artist.*
*One of us wears pearls;*
*the other wears dreadlocks.*
*Different styles, shared values.*

*We think big. We do our homework.*
*We'd choose love over logic any day.*
*We love a good deal.*

*We have branded companies and rallied causes;*
*designed Web sites and books and business plans.*
*We have styled homes and styled people,*
*and what we know for sure is that*

### style is a language.

*We help people to* articulate.

*We inspire authenticity.*

*We see possibility everywhere.*

—C & D

# CONTENTS

8 MANIFESTO OF STYLE

10 A MAP OF THE JOURNEY

## 1
### EXPLORE

14 THIS IS AN INVITATION

18 THIS IS YOUR BOOK

21 REFINED TREASURE
CARRIE McCARTHY

27 SACRED DRAMATIC
DANIELLE LaPORTE

34 INSPIRATION & AUTHENTICITY

36 USING THIS BOOK

39 CHERISHED PLAYFUL
PATSY DUGGAN

44 THE PURPOSE OF A
STYLE STATEMENT:
MAKING POWERFUL CHOICES

48 YOUR STYLE STATEMENT IS...

51 ORGANIC TREASURE
CANDIS HOEY

56 THE 80/20 STYLE
STATEMENT PRINCIPLE:
THE POWER OF PROPORTION

61 CULTIVATED STORY
LYLE REIMER
TIMELESS CONSTRUCTIVE
RAYMOND BOUTET

66 FREQUENTLY ASKED
QUESTIONS

69 CONTEMPORARY FLOURISH
LEISA WASHINGTON

76 WHAT IS STYLE?

79 GENUINE LEGACY
DONALD CLIFTON McMILLAN III

## 2
### INQUIRE

86 WELCOME TO THE
INQUIRY PROCESS

88 THE LIFESTYLE MAP

90 STYLE STRETCH: AN INQUIRY

92 STYLE RUN: AN INQUIRY

95 SIMPLY CRAFTED
SU T FITTERMAN

100 THE SPIRIT AND
LOOK & FEEL OF YOUR LIFE...

105 CONSTRUCTIVE PLAYFUL
KLEE LARSEN

110 HOME + STUFF

117 GENUINE ELEGANCE
AUDREY BEAULAC

122 FASHION + SENSUALITY

129 CURRENT SENSUAL
NAVJIT KANDOLA

134 SPIRIT + LEARNING

141 INNOVATIVE FEMININE
MELODY BIRINGER

# 3

## DEFINE

146 SERVICE + WEALTH

153 ENDURING BOLD
KATE STEVENSON
DESIGNED EASE
ANDREW WILLIAMSON

158 RELATIONSHIPS +
COMMUNICATION

165 NATURAL COSMOPOLITAN
VICTORIA ROBERTS
FEMININE DRAMATIC
DOROTHEA ROBERTS

170 CREATIVITY + CELEBRATION

177 GENTEEL VITALITY
JOAN PHAM

182 BODY + WELLNESS

189 CLASSIC HARMONY
LYN CONNOCK

194 NATURE + REST &
RELAXATION

202 DEFINING YOUR
STYLE STATEMENT

206 THE 80/20
STYLE STATEMENT
PRINCIPLE: A REFRESHER

208 IT'S ALL ABOUT YOU:
DEFINING YOUR STYLE STATEMENT

# 4

## DESIGN

218 DESIGNING YOUR LIFE:
SEE IT, FEEL IT, BE IT

220 PERSPECTIVES & PRACTICE:
50 WAYS TO EXPRESS YOUR STYLE
STATEMENT

224 5 GUIDING QUESTIONS

225 3 SIMPLE THINGS A WEEK

226 ASK YOURSELF:
A JOURNALING EXERCISE

228 A FEW REMINDERS

230 LIFE WALK-THROUGH

232 GO FORTH AND LIVE AS ART!

## STYLE VOCABULARY+

234 FOUNDATION WORDS

252 CREATIVE EDGE WORDS

254 ASK-A-FRIEND SURVEY

255 GRATITUDE

256 BEHIND THE SCENES

Carrie & Danielle's

# Manifesto of Style

1. **Communicate who you are in all you do.** Consistency is power. When the various parts of your life reflect your essence, your life moves in the direction you want it to.

2. **Style is multidimensional.** Visual and sensual choices are driven by self-perception. Our image is a composite of our beliefs, history, and desires.

3. **Style matters.** The design of your life can inspire you or mire you. Every aesthetic and material choice sends a message to the world about who you are, and the world responds accordingly.

4. **Authenticity is energizing, economical, and efficient.** The better you know yourself, the clearer your choices. Self-awareness leads to true style.

5. **Accentuate the positive.** Give your attention to the best in you and around you, and the best will flourish.

6. **People are like snowflakes—uniquely beautiful because of the details.** To compare snowflakes is not very productive. Instead, celebrate what sets you apart, what's most particular and true for you, and your own specialness will become clear.

7. **Pay attention to what attracts you.** One of the most powerful questions you can ask is, what am I drawn to?

8. **Working from the outside in can create deep transformation.** Surface changes have the power to alter your inner landscape. (So yes, sometimes a new hairstyle or a work of art can change your life.)

9. **Feel free to change.** When you discover something true about yourself, put it into action, regardless of who you were yesterday.

10. **True style is not dependent on wealth, and wealth does not necessarily create taste.** Authenticity is not dependent on funding. On a budget, or on easy street, you owe it to yourself to find a way to be genuinely you.

11. **Cheap is expensive in the long run.** Why buy twice when you can buy once? Commit to quality and it will commit to you.

12. **Use your best every day.** Life is too short to wait for a special occasion to bring out your finery, your treasures, your brilliance, and the best of your love.

13. **Choose from your heart, and your life will fill up with things you love.** What works is what feels right.

14. **Beauty transforms.** Its capacity to generate pleasure, healing, and connection is divinely powerful. Beauty affects its maker and beholder every time.

15. **It's always a good time to be yourself.** And it's never too late. Possibility exists all of the time, everywhere. You haven't missed your chance to be your most beautiful.

16. **Only love is free—everything else costs.** Whether it's with time, space, emotion, or earthly resources, we pay for what we choose. Be selective about what you need.

17. **Creativity + restraint = beauty.** Overdone style leaves little room for newness, appreciation, or reciprocity. Hold back a bit. Allow for breathing space. Trust in the power of subtlety.

18. **Contrast makes things interesting.** Too much sameness dulls the senses. Create a twist.

19. **Living is sensual.** Engage life with all you've got.

20. **Make more choices—moment to moment, day to day.** You are the designer of your life. Be selective, creative, and intentional in every possible way.

# A Map of the Journey

**EXPLORE: PART 1**

The first part of this book is an introduction to the many expressions of style. Here, we hope you'll begin to recognize that style is much, much more than what you wear and that authenticity is a mighty powerful lifestyle concept.

The Style Statement profiles and snapshots are beautiful and inspiring views but also instructive true stories about how a Style Statement is reflected in one's life.

**INQUIRE: PART 2**

This is the must-do to part of the trip. First, you can warm up your creative thinking and ease into some self-exploration with the Style Stretch questions on page 90 and the Style Run on page 92.

Things really kick into gear within the Inquiry sections. There are eight of them, each based on a part of the Lifestyle Map (see page 89). Every section asks you to reflect on and respond to questions about what works well and what does not work for you in the fundamental areas of your life.

**DEFINE: PART 3**

In the Style Statement formula, you will literally filter your answers through the defining process. Here you will **collect the key words, concepts, and themes** that have shown up in your "What works well for me" and "What does not work for me" responses.

In this phase, the Style Vocabulary and **a dictionary and thesaurus** are essential tools.

The naming process requires both reason and emotion. There is a logic to follow, and, at the same time, each choice needs to resonate with your heart. It's helpful to be focused *and* open, intentional *and* playful. Your Style Statement may come to you in a flash, or you may need to do some chiseling to find the right shape. When we are open and discerning, we make space for the right things to show up and allow the wrong things to slip away. So breathe. Relax. Play. And remember that you are in charge.

## DESIGN: PART 4

We mean *design* in the multidimensional sense, of course. Part 4 offers a menu of perspectives and practices that encourage you to use your Style Statement as a tool for intentionally designing every aspect of your life.

## STYLE VOCABULARY+

For the sake of convenience, we've tucked the reference materials—the Style Vocabulary and the Ask-a-Friend Survey—at the back of the book.

**Foundation Words** reflect common, almost archetypal themes for many of us and can be used to describe *both* the material and the immaterial. So it's likely that one of these words could become the first word of your Style Statement, your 80%. This list is by no means exhaustive. We encourage you—in fact we implore you—to find the words that best fit your spirit. Feel free to explore words beyond those that appear in our list.

**Creative Edge Words** can be applied to the **spirit and look & feel** of someone or something. This list may be especially useful for choosing the second word of your Style Statement, which represents your 20%. You will need a dictionary to look up the meanings of these words. A thesaurus might also be helpful. Again, there are worlds of other possible words that could fit you, so keep your mind wide open.

The **Ask-a-Friend Survey** is a small questionnaire that you can send to someone close to you to get their perspective on *you.*

The privilege of a lifetime is being who you are.

—JOSEPH CAMPBELL

# Explore

## Part 1

# THIS IS AN
# INVIT

Do you look like yourself?

               Are you at home in your life?

Are you living by your own design?

Women and men, CEOs and civil servants, fashionistas and fashionphobes, full-time mamas and emerging entrepreneurs—for everyone who wants to sharpen their personal edge, steer steady through transitions, or reclaim their mojo, this is a call to inspired and authentic living.

Your Style Statement defines
your authentic self.

It is a compass for making more
powerful choices, a guide for designing
a life that reflects your whole being.

An anchor, a symbol, a mantra.
A declaration, an affirmation, a reminder.


You, fully expressed.

Knowing your Style Statement helps you make empowered decisions—from your wardrobe and home to your relationships and work. When the spirit and the look and feel of your life are connected to your true nature, you feel at home wherever you are. You walk taller. You think more clearly. And the world responds accordingly.

A STYLE STATEMENT INTEGRATES THE VARIOUS ASPECTS OF YOUR BEING IN AN EFFECTIVE BALANCE. IT CONSISTS OF TWO WORDS: THE FIRST WORD IS YOUR FUNDAMENTAL NATURE, 80% OF WHO YOU ARE. THE SECOND WORD IS YOUR CREATIVE EDGE, YOUR DISTINCTION, THE 20% OF YOURSELF THAT MAKES ALL THE DIFFERENCE.

In a materialistic culture obsessed with image, it can be hard to stay in touch with your real self. Amid the craze of "bigger, better, faster," living real takes some determination. You must navigate through big brands, and the "reality" of prime time, not to mention corporate policy, grown-up peer pressure, and things you have dragged with you from your past. All too often, your best self gets buried beneath conformity and confusion. You wonder if the true you—the juicy, life-loving, most dynamic parts of you—can be excavated, refurbished, and finally pulled together all in one place.

We're here to tell you that you're not missing a thing. You have everything you need to be whole. Your desires, your genius, your quirks, and your confusion are the pathways to your treasures. There is gold within.

In a world where authenticity is in short supply, a Style Statement is a tool for genuine and, therefore, more effective expression. From your love to your living room, your talents to your promises, **communicating who you are in all you do is very powerful stuff.**

# THIS IS YOUR

Identifying your Style Statement is a walk down memory lane, a 360-degree tour of your present, and a blue-sky flight into your future. Like any journey worth taking, a sense of adventure and curiosity is essential.

**Appearances run deep.** If you want an energized life, in full color, with surround sound, you've got to dive into yourself. Only the self-referencing thrive. We rarely think twice about what we're attracted to. But what floats our boat—and *why*—is the zillion-dollar question.

Everything matters. Consider it all. Where else will you have a chance to analyze your choices in shoes *and* in relationships, or your idea of sexy *and* your definition of genius?

For some, this book will be a deep dive into your inner self and the power of your preferences. For others, it will be an exercise in stretching your self-expression and more fully celebrating your creativity. Whether revolutionizing or refining—no matter where you're at—you're bound to get clearer on how you got here and where you want to go.

Cling to simplicity,
sincerity, serenity,
and the power of truth.

—I CHING

BOOK

**A TRUE STORY**

**This book, quite literally, will be a defining moment for you.** We name our
pets and our children; we assume married names; and we take on zodiac signs
and the labels assigned to us in personality tests. Spiritual names and dignified
titles are even bestowed on some of us. But it's not often that we distinguish
ourselves with profound and directive meaning.

**This is an opportunity to define yourself on your own terms.** Creating your
own Style Statement is a powerful act of self-determination. Whether you are
living in disguise, or living out loud, we believe that to name your nature in this
way is to embrace your greatest potential.

**The most powerful story you can tell is your own.** Yet we rarely step back from
our lives to review our own biographies. Everybody's everyday story is as layered
and as large as any on the silver screen. There is no such thing as "bigger than life."
What could be bigger than life? Life is big! *Your* life is big! In addition to dates,
locations, and circumstance, life is a tapestry of talents and longings, of questions
and choices. This is your storybook—with an ending that is just the beginning.

# REFINED
## TREASURE

# Carrie McCarthy, January 1959

*Designer. Searcher. Seer.*

## Refined

**SPIRIT:** Refined is dignified, at ease, well mannered, and a touch old-fashioned. Good taste is at the top of their list. Refined is intentional and prefers to strategize, review things, and have a plan. Punctuality is a must, and precision is the intention. Refined likes to redesign, reorganize, replenish, purify, perfect, polish, refine. They are self-assured, and no matter the circumstances emanate class and dignity, usually suggesting ease or wealth—in spirit or materially. They strive for purity—in food, behavior, colors, and surroundings—and avoid things that are distasteful, tacky, rugged, and crude. On a bad day, Refined can be slightly prudish or snooty. They appreciate a sense of history, thoughtful presentation, and values-based living. They aim for impeccability and don't waste time or energy on things or situations that are below their level of idealism and quality, though they will always decline or depart in the most gracious way possible.

**LOOK & FEEL:** Polished, poised, put together. Sophisticated, classic, traditional, elegant; clean lines, from crisp and tailored to graceful and fluid. Ranges from old world to contemporary design. Smooth, not coarse. Purified, refined materials. Also organic materials, raw minerals, polished finishes.

## Treasure

*abundance, adore, admire, applaud, appreciate, beauty, capital, cash, cherish, conserve, darling, dear, dote on, dream, enjoy, esteem, find, gem, honor, idolize, jewel, like, love, praise, preserve, regard, relish, respect, richness, savor, value, worship,`wealth*

**CLOCKWISE:** Sadie's painting, Dad's trophy, brass bracelet from Rebecca, perfume from Cameron, ostrich egg, sculpture, Allessi vase, Mother's pearls.

**I LOVE:** being a twin, being married, the color white, negative space, and teacups. My grandfather's watch and my mother's pearls. The freedom that I feel in nature and in being connected to God. I love my dining room table. It's a hundred-year-old wood table from a convent in Quebec. It's marked and worn and still strong, soaked with stories and meaning.

**I FEEL UNCOMFORTABLE ABOUT MONEY:** when I don't have a plan.

**MY FORM OF EXERCISE:** always involves movement. Feeling free is essential for me. Running in the rain, speed, solitude, breathing space.

**I STAND FOR:** beauty, possibility, a commitment to growing.

**I APPRECIATE:** good manners. Thank-you cards. Affection.

**MY FAVORITE MAGAZINES:** *Domino, Vogue Living,* and *Inc.*

**I AM INSPIRED BY:** ideas and learning; people who achieve against the odds.

**I AM AMAZED BY:** mothers.

**ART THAT HAS MOVED ME:** Alberto Giocometti lithographs, my nieces' drawings and crafts.

**I AM HARDEST ON MYSELF:** when I compare myself to others.

**I FEEL CHERISHED:** when someone really listens.

**MY GUILTY PLEASURE:** Best Foods mayonnaise.

**MY DREAM HOME:** An old Georgian house in the city, with an English garden. And a west coast contemporary house on the Gulf Islands.

**I'D WEAR TO THE ACADEMY AWARDS:** Vionnet dress in silver gray-blue. Layers and strands of pearl necklaces. Outrageously sexy shoes.

***REFINED* MEANS TO ME:** Purity, light, grace.

***TREASURE* MEANS TO ME:** Being in the moment, finding richness in myself and others, hunting the unusual.

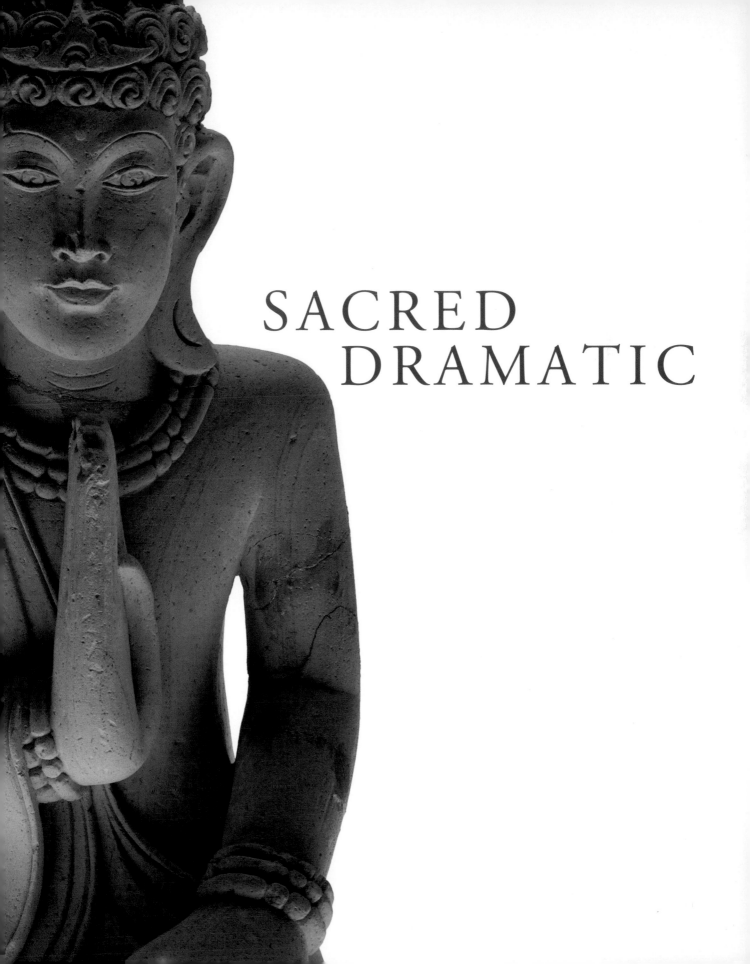

SACRED
DRAMATIC

# Danielle LaPorte, May 1969

*Wife & Mama. Writer. Philanthropist.*

## Sacred

**SPIRIT:** Sacred is philosophically and theologically curious, perpetually searching for or creating meaning. They are habitually reflective, looking for divine synchronicities and lessons in everything. Often the one to initiate change, whether that be a promising beginning or a necessary end, Sacred walks a fine line between ruthless discrimination and tremendous tolerance. Advisers, mavens, and teachers, they reliably appear at the scene of life's big passages and events to bring grace and wit. Sacred loves to mark moments of insight and progress with celebrations small and quiet or grand. They feel and promote interconnectedness and endeavor to be aware of materials, resources, and channels of communication. Sacred nourishes itself by retreating, and takes great solace in privacy and solitude, ritual, and unbounded time. Sacred tends to be singularly focused and intensely devoted to personal values or causes. On a dark day, they can be righteous and critical. With spiritual communion as their core inspiration, Sacred is built to live in service to the whole and longs to do so through their own creative outlets.

**LOOK & FEEL:** Aesthetic is based on more on feelings and stories than literal fashion—anything goes if it is deemed cherished. Asian and Eastern influences; attracted to heritages of many cultures. Lean toward simplistic or graceful design. Try to engage sensuality in all matters: lighting, lyrics, rhythms, scent; warmth, quality fabrics, pure colors, pleasurable tastes.

## Dramatic

*affecting, breathtaking, change agent, climactic, cultivated, effective, elegant, exciting, expressive, forceful, glamorous, impactful, influential, inspired, meaningful, passionate, performer, persuasive, poetic, powerful, results, sensitive, striking, sublime, tasteful, thespian, thrilling, vivid, visible, voice*

**CLOCKWISE:** Passport, retractable fountain pen from Scott, my first Mother's Day gift, nest from Mayne Island, holy water font, sandal, Style Statement ring + wedding ring, mascara, matches (I love fire!)

**THINGS I LOVE:** chunky gold, elegant solutions, velocity, being of service, snuggling.

**FORM OF EXERCISE:** climbing into a hot bath.

**ART THAT HAS MOVED ME:** Mark Rothko's paintings. Jim Morrison's *An American Prayer* recordings—shamanic, drunk, rock poet—makes me hot in every way. Leonard Cohen's concert at Santa Fe's Palo Solari: "There is a crack in everything, that's how the light gets in." Elvis's *'68 Comeback Special!* The set, the gospel, and those perfectly fit leather pants. He knew who he was.

**I ENVY:** trust funds.

**I CRAVE:** heat. Belly laughs. Pineapple. Intimacy.

**FAVORITE FLOWER:** is yet to be discovered. I'm sure it exists somewhere in the desert and only blossoms during a full moon.

**GREATEST ACCOMPLISHMENT:** Our son's home birth.

**BOOKS THAT HAVE DEFINED ME:** *Women Who Run with the Wolves* by Clarissa Pinkola Estés; *The Soul's Code* by James Hillman; *Ask and It Is Given* by Esther and Jerry Hicks; *Envisioning Information* by Edward R. Tufte.

**GUILTY PLEASURE:** *People* magazine.

**VERY INTERESTED IN:** the truth—and everyone's own version of it. Conscious parenting. Pop culture. What my husband wants.

**A SMALL PART OF ME:** wants to shave my head and live in a secluded adobe in New Mexico with my little family and mean ol' pickup truck.

***SACRED* MEANS TO ME:** What you make matter. Communion. Reverence. Respect.

***DRAMATIC* MEANS TO ME:** Feeling things deeply, self-expression, creating impact.

# In Carrie's Words

I spent my twenties pondering my purpose and, for the most part, feeling a sense of disconnectedness. I'm naturally athletic and creative, and I spent years competing as a track runner and eventually studying fashion design. While going to school in London, I was invited by a good friend to a gallery show dedicated exclusively to chairs. "I don't know what the big deal is," I told her. "They're just chairs." But for the first time, I really looked. Each chair was a lesson in history and personality. Design had significance. What a revelation! And I realized that just like I'd trained my body to do more, I could train my eyes to see more.

When I moved into interior design, I experienced more outward success. Wealthy clients. Magazine shoots. Recognition for my work. But I was still plagued with feelings of not being enough. I didn't fit in with the waspy businesspeople who were my clients. And I didn't quite fit in with the artsy, creative people who were my friends, though they inspired me so much. Their creativity was abundant. Gold-washed walls and rich oil paintings. They were Bohemian and risky. *People live like this?* I thought. It was fantastic for me.

With more exposure, my definition of beauty deepened. *Beauty* is hearing other people tell their truth. *Beauty* is drawing pictures, even when you're scared. *Beauty* is asking.

## ASKING

Because I believe so strongly in equality, interior design made me uncomfortable at times. I was working with the haves—have more money, more opportunities, more education. The habit of making comparisons between the haves and have-nots was almost impossible to avoid. But, fortunately, I had a stronger habit, which was to ask. To ask, what is most important? Is there another way? What else is there?

Asking more life-important questions with my interior design clients was organic. The magic question was, how can they know themselves better? And that's how Style Statement was born.

The work of Style Statement made my whole life make sense. What I loved and how I loved. How I presented myself and my creations. All the questions that I'd asked myself, I could now ask others. This was the mode of teaching I'd been looking for. Instead of feeling shallow and lost, I felt full and grounded. Finally, I had beauty *and* meaning. My separate worlds became one.

# In Danielle's Words

I had spent about six months in pajamas. My man and I had moved back to our favorite city to put down roots. I was career fried. I'd just left my job in Washington, DC. As the director of a think tank, riding the swells of the dot-com craze, I needed a break from fast-track global thinking.

Soon after my winter refuge, some new friends tipped me off to Carrie McCarthy. Carrie was looking for guinea pigs for a process she called Style Statement. The timing was more divine than I could have ever imagined.

Carrie arrived at my bungalow in a chic navy jumpsuit. She was incredibly fit, and stylish, in a Ralph Lauren–Upper West Side kind of way. From her big leather bag, she pulled out a pad of graph paper and a few HB pencils. "I'm a little nervous because I've heard how smart you are," she confessed. *You're nervous?* I thought to myself. *Well, I've got a bad Joan Jett haircut, I'm twenty pounds more than myself, and I have no idea who I'm going to be when I grow up. And by the way, I just got out of my pajamas.*

In her gentle, steady way, Carrie began, "Where in the world do you feel most at home? What makes you feel cherished? What's important to you?" I was digging the process. It was reflective; it was meaningful; and it was going somewhere. She scribbled my replies, circled some words, made notes in the margin.

"I think I've got it," she said after about an hour. "I'm wondering if your Style Statement is Sacred Dramatic." I repeated it in my mind: *Sacred... Dramatic.* I was nodding, starting to grin. I felt a bit giddy. "Yeah. Wow... you're *good*." The fire was lit.

Carrie & Danielle

# Inspiration & Authenticity

As creative partners, clearly, one of us is a little bit country and one is a little bit rock 'n' roll. We come from different classes and generations. We work and play differently. And yet, we are woven like the branches of a tree, rooted in our beliefs in the human spirit, the power of gratitude, the purpose of money, and the divine audacity of dreaming big—very big.

Mostly, we love to inspire authenticity, whether through sincere listening or beautiful imagery or new solutions. We think that authenticity is a force for social change—as mighty as solar power and democracy and first love. Authenticity clears the mind and warms the heart. It magnifies and heals and delights. We see it happen every day.

**WE DON'T BELIEVE IN DESTINY, BUT IF WE DID, WE'D SAY WE WERE DESTINED TO BE TOGETHER.**
Style Statement circled around us for a few years while we plodded through the final phases of our careers in interior design and business development. Our friendship grew over new men, weddings, and a baby. We kept gravitating toward each other's talents and ideals, until the inevitable happened. The disenchanted decorator and the jaded consultant became the very liberated Carrie & Danielle, Incorporated.

We kept each other on track as we lived our own Style Statements. *Treasure yourself more. Easy on the Dramatic.* We paid the rent with design work, and in between gigs we wrangled up friends for Style Statement interviews. We offered our services for free. We learned which questions evoked the richest responses. We drew diagrams. We documented our findings. By the time we'd done our hundredth Style Statement, something marvelous had started happening. People were telling their friends.

We were amazed at the range of people who showed up. New moms in the midst of identity crises. Young artists. An executive who wanted his office to better reflect his personality. Retired teachers. Aestheticians. Media personalities. Secretaries and salespeople. Broke, middle class, and millionaires. People wanted pointers toward their lives' purpose. Some of our clients were self-aware, savvy, and confident in most areas of their lives. Others were feeling completely adrift. Without exception, each and every

one of them was seeking clarity and validation. Some of them took a spoonful; some of them left with a year's supply.

The communication opened up. Our Style Statement clients e-mailed to say, "Its working!" We heard about new wardrobes, peace of mind, and big decisions. *I use my Style Statement as a guide for managing my money.... I've started wearing more color....I'm working on a new painting....I've stopped comparing myself to other women....This has made saying no so much easier!*

Of course, we already knew it worked. It was working in our own lives. We were making more Refined and Sacred choices. We were giving more of ourselves every day, and in doing so, our treasures began to grow, with dramatic results.

# Using This Book

**GO YOUR OWN WAY**

Use this book as a guide, a sketchbook, or a sounding board. This is your private studio in which to create. Make notes in the margins; sketch pictures; glue in photos or images that inspire you. Highlight passages; circle favorite words. You do not have to answer every question or work through the sections in any particular order.

**IMPROVISE**

**Think outside your box. Exorcise your past. Laugh at yourself, and admit to a few bad choices. Above all, think highly of yourself.**

This is not a test or an aptitude exam or an intelligence quiz. And it is certainly not an assessment of how cool or fashionable you are. It is a creative experience—one part art, one part science—an inquiry into the many dimensions of your character and constitution.

Many personality tests can determine with great accuracy what might motivate or repel you, but they give little or no insight into your aesthetic values and tastes. And fashion quizzes that peg you as "Sporty" or "Chic" won't be of much use when choosing your career path or wellness regimen. This book is the place where your psychology is matched to your shoes, and your higher self becomes your personal shopper. *Style Statement* is where mind *and* matter meet. **Mostly, this book is an opportunity for you to be seen and heard by the most important person in your life—you.**

### OPEN YOUR MIND

As you swim through the likes and dislikes that each inquiry section asks you to explore, what rises to the surface might surprise you. Be open. Try to suspend any preconceived notions you may have about yourself, and be willing to experience a few "wow" moments: *Wow, I can see how much I value reliability. Wow, I need much more freedom than I'm getting.*

*Wow, I am stronger than I've given myself credit for.* The more honest you are with yourself in this process, the more you will learn and the more effectual your Style Statement will become.

**Perhaps your inner self has been throwing you clues for years, and you've been too busy to get the hint.** Maybe, just maybe, who you really are and how you perceive and present yourself are miles apart, in which case, your Style Statement could come as quite a surprise—and a relief.

This is more about discovering yourself than it is about labeling yourself. Discovery is about finding resources, hidden strengths, and treasures. Labeling, on the other hand, suggests that you find something outside yourself and apply it. Labels can conceal. Discovery reveals.

# CHERISHED
# PLAYFUL

Patsy Duggan, February 1946

*Tourism Specialist. Event Planner. Caregiver.*

## Cherished

**SPIRIT:** A collector of friends, experiences, and well-worn things; when Cherished loves you, you know it. Cherished is deeply sentimental, though not necessarily stuck in the past, because Cherished is always endeavoring to create new life experiences and memories. They love to celebrate, venture out, and bring good people and worthy causes together. Cherished adores hearing or telling a good story and have plenty of them to share. Natural and gleeful caretakers, Cherished has an abundance of nurturing energy and affection, which is generously given to strengthen and sustain. They can be generous to a fault and need to remember that they do not have to save the world—caring for themselves first and foremost is a great way to be of service. With an unshakable values system and moral compass, Cherished can be remarkably determined and focused. Love is its strength.

**LOOK & FEEL:** If there's a story behind it, it works for Cherished! Nostalgic, sentimental, culturally rich, and diverse. Personalized, attention to detail, inviting. Because Cherished can be both "in the moment" and "in the past," fashion and decor can be a combination of the simple and contemporary, vintage and old world.

## Playful

*adventuresome, amusing, artful, cheerful, clever, coy, creative, entertaining, fanciful, good-natured, happy, humorous, ironic, irreverent, joyous, lighthearted, lively, mischievous, recreating, relaxating, satirical, saucy, smart, spirited, vivacious, whimsical, witty*

**CLOCKWISE:** Rice bowl—I eat dinner from it every night; my everywhere cap, Art Deco triptych mirror from an old boyfriend, yoga mats, shoe, my signature lipstick, dress from my socialite auntie, faith stone from Nelson

**I LOVE:** where I live. The thrill of travel. Spending time with my daughter (she's my best friend). My grandkids. Moving water. Matinees. Cream-colored clothing and furniture. Cappuccinos. Yoga class. Some glass hearts from friends. My French armoire.

**MOST RIDICULOUS PURCHASE THAT I EVER MADE:** I was training for a marathon, and as I ran through downtown, I couldn't resist jogging right into Max Mara. I fell in love with a coat and ran eight miles back home to get my credit card. And once, I sold my house to afford to go to India. It turned out not to be that ridiculous!

**MY IDEA OF A DISASTROUS FIRST DATE:** I could get a laugh out of anything, so really, there are no disasters. It is what it is.

**WHAT'S WORKING IN MY WARDROBE:** I'm having fun with cropped pants, kneesocks, and fabulous black boots. My sweater coat and English wool hat. A holster bag with a cell phone pocket in the front.

**SOMETHING I'D LIKE TO HAVE MADE FOR ME:** A wedding dress.

**I CRAVE:** love and generosity.

**I NOURISH MY WELL-BEING:** with yoga, massage, acupuncture, meditation.

**MY LIFE PURPOSE IS:** to bring love and abundance to the world—to everybody. I'd like to be in India working with service organizations—that is what I'm working toward.

**I HAVE VERY LITTLE TOLERANCE FOR:** unnecessary rudeness.

**I LOOK MY MOST FABULOUS:** when I'm in the presence of my son. And when I was at my daughter's wedding, I was glowing with happiness!

**MY FAVORITE SCENTS:** Lavender and lime.

***CHERISHED* MEANS TO ME:** Integrity. Everything present in my life has a story behind it. I cherish every moment of every day because who knows about tomorrow.

***PLAYFUL* MEANS TO ME:** Enjoying whatever it is that I'm doing.

# The Purpose of a
# Style Statement:
# Making Powerful Choices

*I wish I'd said what I really wanted to say.*

*All day I wanted to go home and change my outfit.*

*I knew in my gut that the project wasn't a good fit.*

*I feel like an imposter, and I'm worried they'll find me out.*

*Spent too much again.*

*Cheaped out again.*

*What the hell was I thinking?*

There's no way around it—being out of sync with yourself sucks. The wrong words or environment or packaging can feel like an itchy blanket on your truly tender spirit—warm for a minute but incredibly irritating after a while. **When you are adrift from your core, the space between your surface and your depth fills up with anxiety.** Too much time away from your inner home leads to homesickness.

Danish philosopher Søren Kierkegaard considered anxiety a valuable tool for shaping our ideal lives. He believed that the remedy for anxiety is choosing to be the self that we truly are. We couldn't agree more. But *choosing* isn't always easy.

**Society sets us up to be right or wrong and rewards us accordingly.** This is the very nature of culture and tribe. There is nothing especially restrictive about the times we are living in—in fact, in many ways today we are freer to be ourselves than we have ever been. But humans instinctively seek approval and comfort, so dualism—right vs. wrong, them vs. us, and more vs. less—is the lens through which we view both our outer and inner worlds.

**We desire to belong *and* to be seen for who we are.** This is the most divine paradox of human nature. The sweetest possibilities for fulfillment live within the creative tensions of *me and us and them.*

The problem is not within society's codes of conduct, traditions, or cultural values—all of which potentially hold greatly self-affirming and life-enhancing principles. Life starts to get problematically dull when we fail to look within, when we lose touch with our own sense of what feels right or wrong. When we feed ourselves a diet of ideas about success and happiness that other people have cooked up, then our genuine character begins to starve and we make weak choices about what we bring into our lives and put out into the world.

**We are trained to keep up—and call ourselves achievers.** Higher grades, better looks, faster car. Bigger house, bigger bonus, bigger boobs. Big and fast might be fabulous, but these pleasures and prizes can only bring deep delight if you are making self-guided choices, in harmony with your true nature.

**The good news is that we have more to choose from than ever before! The bad news is that we have more to choose from than ever before!** If you're disconnected from your center, it's easy to be swept away by the thousands of sensory messages you receive on a daily basis, many of them strategically personalized to target your zip code and other personal statistics. Each dollar you spend unconsciously and every forced decision you make lets a little piece of your power out the door.

# Are You the Individual That You Think You Are?

*Gay, straight, divorced, single parent. Vegetarian, tattooed, pierced, promiscuous. Conservative. Liberal. Passive-aggressive. Highly sensitive. Bohemian. Eco warrior. Geek.* To further complicate the "privilege of being who you are," we live in an era when it's cool to be special. Being an individual is the norm. That's right. It is now normal to be different. How's that for paradox and pressure?

Liberating yourself does not necessarily mean that you have to barrel toward the fringes of the mainstream or claw your way up the corporate ladder. Sometimes it's wise to suit up and shut up. Company dress codes, annual taxes, common courtesies—some kinds of conformity can be beautifully righteous and purposeful.

Ironically, when you know who you are on the inside, it can be much easier to roll with outside forces. Unexamined conformity, on the other hand, is downright lazy. Choice is like a muscle. If you work it enough, you make stronger decisions—decisions that carry you forward in the direction of your dreams.

**To combat overstimulation, overconsumption, and overwhelment, you have to be ruthlessly committed to who you really are. Unwaveringly devoted. Loyally, royally you.**

It helps to be reminded just how terrifically "you" you are. Positive reinforcement will light a fire in your belly and get you across the finish line almost every time.

And that's just what a **Style Statement is—positive reinforcement.** A Style Statement is a compass for making more powerful choices.

# Choose You

A powerful choice is one that honors your mind, body, and soul.

Every day is filled with opportunities to choose powerfully. So instead of feeling just shy of your potential, uncomfortable in your own skin, or like a big fat fake, you can use the truth of your Style Statement to steer toward the big-as-life you. And then you may hear yourself saying some incredible things:

*I love what I do.*

*I feel so alive when I wear this color.*

*I'm taking salsa lessons, and I feel so sexy!*

*My home is my sanctuary.*

*I called it like I saw it.*

*I saved a fortune.*

*I made a fortune.*

*That's so me.*

# Your Style Statement is...

Your Style Statement is an affirmation, a declaration, a symbol of the real you—and all your facets. But what if you're unsure about which parts of yourself to reinforce or accentuate or give voice to? What if your own values and desires or your reality and ideals are seemingly in conflict? Like the MBA who wants to be a stay-at-home mom, or the sexy dresser with old-fashioned morals? Or the eco-friendly yoga teacher who wants to be a millionaire?

There is no right or wrong way to be yourself. The basis of authenticity is acceptance. Authenticity has many interpretations. Sometimes, being real means being true to your heritage. Sometimes it means being true to your current circumstances. Most often, authenticity is simply what feels right.

Even if we have repeatedly repressed or neglected the truest aspect of our being—whether it's spontaneity, gentleness, or our go-get-it mojo—magic can come back into our lives with a sincere invitation or invocation. It's never too late to become the real you.

# All of You

**A Style Statement integrates your essence and your personality.**
Self-expression is not an either-or formula. It is, in Carl Jung's words, "magnificently affirmative of both-and." You can be traditional and avant-garde, opportunistic and socially responsible, serene and flamboyant. It's all good if it's all real. It is infinitely better to be fully yourself with myriad contradictions than to be an indirect, inauthentic version of yourself. Identities are crackled, colorful kaleidoscopes. And it's the whole package of talents and flaws and preferences that make us infinitely more interesting.

**A Style Statement is a guide, a focal point, a mantra for making choices about the look, feel, and spirit of every area of your life.** In a consumer-driven society that overloads us with must-haves and must-dos, your Style Statement is a grounding rod. You'll have far fewer *what was I thinking?* moments. Consider your Style Statement a direct line to your inner wisdom and better judgment.

**Using your Style Statement as a guide creates ease and efficiency in your life.** Confusion is a time suck, and weak decisions can be costly. With inner clarity, you stop wasting time, energy, and money striving to be what and who others—be they media, community, or family—tell you to be.

**Applying your Style Statement generates confidence and consistency, which build power and momentum.** As your good choices begin to add up, so will your trust in your own perspective and abilities. A sense of continuity and flow will become part of your regular experience.

Authenticity is a force of nature. When you channel it to intentionally design the look and feel of every aspect of your life, your outsides begin to match your insides. And something truly magical happens. You continue to become more genuinely yourself, and you have more of what you want.

ORGANIC
TREASURE

## Candis Hoey, September 1967

*Mom. Hairstylist. Aspiring Writer.*

### Organic

**SPIRIT:** Organic is a divine dichotomy: practical but spontaneous, structured but flowing. The disposition of Organic is like that of bamboo—light, incredibly strong, growing freely and prolifically. Organic is mindful of the connections between parts, whether in relationships, systems, or physical things. They keenly sense what's going on (never miss a thing!) and what needs to happen in order to create harmony and ease—Organic strives to unify. They are commonsensi-cal, practical, and organized, and adore systems and solutions that simplify or create ease and efficiency. The challenge for Organic is to accept change without overthinking it, to trust what they already know is true. Organic is wholesome with pure intentions. Their feet are on the ground, and they are in tune with the natural order, seasons, and stages of living and working.

**LOOK & FEEL:** Organic's aesthetic is based on sensuality, quality, and construc-tion—whether structured or flowing, shape is important. Timeless or simplis-tic styles, and handcrafted, socially responsible or eco-friendly materials. Layered aromas, rich textures, enduring and natural fabrics and substances; hearty and sturdy; never static, always changing; free from manufacturing, over-processing, and chemicals. Pure, essential, enduring.

### Treasure

*abundance, adore, admire, applaud, appreciate, beauty, capital, cash, cherish, conserve, darling, dear, dote on, dream, enjoy, esteem, find, gem, honor, idolize, jewel, like, love, praise, preserve, regard, relish, respect, richness, savor, value, worship, wealth*

THE
PROPHET
by
KAHLIL GIBRAN

CLOCKWISE: Organic sage, sandalwood incense (smells like pure earth), home-baked scone, *The Prophet* by Kahlil Gibran, heart and crown locket from Tim (elegant meets badass), 501 Levi's, shawl from D's trip to India, fancy sea salt

**I LOVE:** coffee, beautiful homes, organic tomatoes off the vine, the beach, my kids, bakeries, bookstores, incense, red wine, cheese, cookbooks, galleries, money, the weight of good linen, clean bathrooms. Geminis, because their dry sense of humor makes me laugh.

**ARTISTS WHO HAVE MOVED ME:** My husband. I'm so impressed with the continuity in his work. And Frank Gehry. Seeing his exhibit was a turning point for me.

**I SECRETLY LOVE:** my Levi's 501 cutoffs and my old army boots.

**SMELLS:** are fundamental to me. Sandalwood, patchouli, rosewood. I am so tuned into fine essential oils because they come from the oldest trees and flowers of the earth. Being able to extract these botanicals and bring them into my home and wear them is a gift that makes me feel connected.

**MY SANCTUARY IS:** my bathtub. Solo herbaceous overload! My baths are total concoctions of bubbles, color therapy, yummy oils. No reading material. No music. Just me in the zone.

**MY IDEA OF AN UNAPPEALING LIVING PLACE:** An uber-modern cube in Manhattan. Zero soul, cookie cutter, can't breathe. Do those windows open?! No grass, no dirt, no oxygen.

**WHEN I DON'T GET ENOUGH R&R:** I become volatile.

**MY PHILOSOPHY ON FRIENDSHIP IS:** borrowed from Kahlil Gibran—let your best be for your friend.

**MY TRIBE IS:** funny and solid—and we're taking new members.

**I AM MY BEST SELF WHEN:** I eat right.

**MY FAVORITE MAGAZINES:** *Real Simple. Ascent. Oprah.*

**I CRAVE:** quality.

**NEGATIVE QUALITIES I CAN HARDLY TOLERATE ARE:** defensiveness and, self-righteousness.

**MY EVIL TWIN IS:** cheap 'n' stingy.

**THE LESSON IN MY LIFE THAT KEEPS REPEATING IS:** to stand in the place where I live.

***ORGANIC* MEANS TO ME:** Of the earth, naturally sourced, edible; appeals to all of my senses; sensual, pure, sincere.

***TREASURE* MEANS TO ME:** Handpicked; I choose you!

# The 80/20 Style Statement Principle

THE POWER OF

PROPO

*Proportion* is defined as the agreeable relation of parts within a whole, or the appropriate combination of elements.

If we find parts of ourselves or our desires in conflict or off-kilter, the 80/20 Style Statement Principle can help create balance and integration. This is the magic formula that makes your Style Statement a truly useful tool. The first word of your Style Statement reflects your inner foundation, your 80%. The second word is your creative edge, your 20%. This combination of energy, ideals, and aesthetics is a powerful equation for creating ease and results in life.

# Your Foundation is your 1st word—your 80%.

### SPIRIT

» Your first word describes your inner foundation, which is your essence, the fundamental you. This is the core of you that feels like **first nature**, innate and implicit.

» Your foundation is your **"being."**

» Your foundation is **what** you are.

» This symbolizes your **roots**.

» Being disconnected from your foundation is uncomfortable and **disorienting**.

» Too much foundation can create inflexibility or righteousness.

### LOOK & FEEL

» Your foundation word works as your basics do—like your suit or your dress, your essential clothing pieces. It may represent the overall style of your home, or it could speak to the big pieces or elements of your living space, like the style of your couch or the building materials and surfaces in a room.

80%

# Your Creative Edge is your 2nd word—your 20%.

## 20%

### SPIRIT

» Your second word describes your creative edge, which is connected to your outer **image** and persona. This word typically represents the **impression** that we'd like to make or the experience we'd like to create.

» Your creative edge is **how you express** your being.

» Your creative edge is **how you do what you do.**

» This symbolizes your **wings.**

» Being disconnected from your creative edge creates a sense of **emptiness** or flatness.

» Too much creative edge can lead to overwhelment or burnout.

» Your second word represents the gift that you long to give the world, as well as the gift that you long to receive.

### LOOK & FEEL

» Your creative edge works as your accessories do. It is the flourish of your fashion. It may be the finishing touches, or color or pattern of an outfit, a space, or any design or product. It's the special twist that brings things to life. Just a touch will do.

# CULTIVATED
# STORY

# TIMELESS
# CONSTRUCTIVE

## Lyle Reimer, March 1978
*Fashion Designer, Evan & Dean.*

## Raymond Boutet, January 1973
*Fashion Designer, Evan & Dean.*

### Cultivated

SPIRIT: Cultivated takes tremendous pleasure in seeing things grow. They love to nurture their inner life, other people, animals, nature, and ultimately good ideas. Happy to foster and promote the growth of others, Cultivated works toward what is best for the individual as well as the group. They are interesting to other people precisely because they are actively and sincerely interested in the world around them. They respect, honor, and celebrate the customs of various communities and traditions and are consummate connectors of people. They are natural leaders. Positively passionate about growing, learning, and teaching, Cultivated is often well trained or educated (either formally or self-taught) and thus can sometimes be quite self-critical, overextending for accomplishments. They always have some pursuit or exploration under way. Cultivated considers all of life's experiences—positive and negative—nutrients for the inner garden from which they reap their harvest.

LOOK & FEEL: Always quality, with a high degree of taste. Can run the gamut from sophisticated and refined to culturally diverse, eccentric, or bohemian. Rich, artistic, intellectually advanced. Full range of textures, tastes, and aromas.

### Story

*adventure, allegory, anecdote, beat, biography, book, comedy, chronicle, description, diary, drama, dramatic, epic, fable, fairy tale, fantasy, feature, fiction, folktale, history, journal, legend, meaning, memoir, myth, narrative, nonfiction, novel, parable, purpose, recital, record, relation, report, romance, saga, scoop, tale*

### Timeless

SPIRIT: Timeless is deeply interested in philosophies, ideas, customs, stories, and objects that have stood the test of time. They pride themselves on their loyalty and staying power and seek to endure with grace. Somewhat sentimental, they choose quality and avoid trendiness and gimmicks; they would rather have a few quality relationships or possessions than numerous less-than-amazing friendships or things. With a long-term focus, Timeless is willing to delay gratification and chooses not to rush. When stressed or strained, they will react in one of two ways: either clinging to structure and regimen, or waffling and flaking out. Independent spirits but inclusive and community-oriented thinkers, they consider who and what has come before and what is being created for the future. Their motto is Quality + Endurance = Luxuriousness.

LOOK & FEEL: Sophisticated, classic, traditional, elegant; polished, clean lines; from crisp and tailored to graceful, fluid, and comfortable; ranges from old world to contemporary design. Solid, quality; durable or very refined textiles. Never goes out of style.

### Constructive

*adorning, advancing, artistic, beautifying, beneficial, broadening, civilizing, corrective, crafted, designed, developmental, dignifying, disciplining, educational, elevating, enlightening, enriching, expanding, helpful, influential, innovative, inspirational, instructive, liberal, nurturing, positive, practical, promoting, refined, regenerative, socializing, stimulating, structured, timely, uplifting, useful, valuable*

## LYLE

**ONE OF MY MOST INSPIRING ARTISTIC EXPERIENCES:** Cirque du Soleil! It is one of my favorite things in the world. It is so amazing to see what the creative mind can achieve.

**I LONG FOR:** success with Evan & Dean—to be an internationally recognized clothing label on par with Gucci.

**THE PERSON WHO KNOWS ME BEST:** is Raymond. He says that I am the most loving person he's known.

**I CRAVE:** honesty; people who are real.

**I AM MY BEST SELF:** when I'm with my family.

**FAVORITE WORD:** Love. The first word I learned to spell was my name. The second was love. As a child I wrote Lyle love...Lyle love everywhere.

**FAVORITE FORM OF PLAY:** Dinner parties.

***CULTIVATED* MEANS TO ME:** Creating your own evolution to further the growth of what's happening around you.

***STORY* MEANS TO ME:** The creative, underlying story that needs to be present in all I do.

## RAYMOND

**I AM INSPIRED BY:** the world around me. Tom Ford for Gucci, Galiano, Lagerfeld, Lyle's use of color, Anne Rice, science fiction. Dreaming about what the future could be.

**I ADMIRE:** my father, for his brilliance—his way of always saying something in just the right way—and his bravery. My mother, for her ability to question and change.

**I HAVE LITTLE TOLERANCE FOR:** vindictiveness and sloppiness.

**I AM ATTRACTED TO:** Lyle. Richness of color, depth, high-contrast items, structure.

**BEAUTY IS:** the world around me. Resting and relaxing.

**MY FRIENDS:** miss me.

**THE PERSON WHO KNOWS MF BEST:** is Lyle. He would say that I always throw something unexpected into the mix.

**MY GIFT TO GIVE:** Kindness—plenty of kindness.

***TIMELESS* MEANS TO ME:** Never ending. Always there.

***CONSTRUCTIVE* MEANS TO ME:** Building.

**CLOCKWISE:** Our favorite magazine, favorite fruit, Old Spice deodorant, Keihl's lotions, Crocs, Herb Ritts's book, *Star Trek* and *Sex and the City* DVDs, elderflower water

# Frequently Asked Questions

Questions, wonderings, curiosities? Allow us to assist you.

### HOW CAN TWO WORDS DEFINE SO MUCH OF ME?

A single word can distill all that you know to be good, beautiful, and true. Words carry energy. Every word has its own history and momentum. It is the result of cultural enterprise, constructed over time. Look into a word, and you will find a world of meaning and possibility. Applied with intention, words are magic formulas.

Arranged in their 80/20 combination (which you can read more about on page 58), your first and second Style Statement words encapsulate the ideal look, feel, and spirit of how you move through the world.

### CAN TWO WORDS GUIDE MY LIFE?

Your Style Statement is a tool. Tools are only useful when you use them. And learning to make a new tool do what you want it to do can take some practice. If you apply your Style Statement to your decision making, creativity, and ways of relating to yourself and others, then yes, unequivocally, your two words can guide your life in the direction that you want it to go. With a guiding hand, it only takes a small rudder to steer a ship.

### WHAT IF I'M CHANGEABLE AND I LIKE TO EXPRESS MYSELF IN LOTS OF DIFFERENT WAYS?

There is always a through line to our personal stories, no matter how many scene changes we make. Behind every choice, as different as those choices may appear to be, are deep longings and talents that are rooted in our spirit. So, on the surface you may be constantly altering your image or your direction, but if you look more deeply into your varied interests, jobs, relationships, or clothes, you will inevitably see themes running through your decisions.

Your Style Statement anchors you to your essence, which can be expressed truthfully in endless ways.

### WHAT IF I'M FASHIONABLE, STYLISH, AND HAPPY WITH MY LOOK?

Terrific. A Style Statement encompasses the look, feel, and spirit of who you really are. It is about more than how you dress or decorate; it is about how you relate and create in every area of living.

### WHAT IF I HAVE NO INTEREST IN FASHION?

Well, then we have to ask, *why not?* Fashion matters. It's an unavoidable fact of our culture. Humans are sensory creatures, and the way we suit up and show up speaks volumes. Having a Style Statement is not about being a fashion plate. It is about defining what's authentic to you and sending clear signals.

### WHAT IF I DON'T "GET" MY STYLE STATEMENT?

There are many ways to engage in this process, and if you're feeling stuck, then there are many ways to get unstuck. Community and shared experiences are great dissolvers of blocks, and you can find that with a group or a friend. Sometimes, just a slight shift in perspective can create a breakthrough, allowing you to find the ideal words that speak to your soul. Also keep in mind that there are many learning opportunities here. Every answer is a gift you give to yourself.

### WHAT IF MY FRIENDS DON'T AGREE WITH MY STYLE STATEMENT?

Your Style Statement is meant to inform and guide you, not the people around you. Sometimes our friends can see us more clearly than we see ourselves, and their perspective is incredibly valuable. And sometimes it's best to say *thanks but no thanks* for their input, and keep on walkin'. Follow your heart.

### HOW DOES A STYLE STATEMENT WORK IN PARTNERSHIP AND SHARING SPACE?

Having a hard time reconciling your partner's wagon-wheel coffee table with your floral-patterned sofa? Or balancing your extrovertedness with your partner's reclusive nature? You can each create your own Style Statements, then combine them into one Style Statement for your relationship and shared space. For example, Cultivated Play and Classic Earth could become Cultivated Earth or Classic Play. You'll have to negotiate about what matters most to you, find your common ground, and decide what words feel inspiring or comforting to both of you.

### IS A STYLE STATEMENT THE SAME AS A PERSONAL BRAND?

The popular term *personal branding* describes the strategy of marketing your outer identity for commercial purposes. It can be very useful in the marketplace because it helps you differentiate yourself from the competition. Likewise, a Style Statement can be immensely useful in achieving business success, but it's not solely about packaging yourself to gain appeal. An individual Style Statement works from the inside out. It's about being genuinely you in every dimension of your life.

### WILL MY STYLE STATEMENT CHANGE OVER TIME?

It depends. When we're teens or young adults, it's not always easy to see the fullness of our essence. Often, the truth takes some time, or some breakthroughs, to be revealed. It's not our essence that changes over time but, rather, our ability to see and feel it. As your inner vision improves with experience, it's useful to take stock of how you've changed. You might want to review your Style Statement after a few years or after major periods of transformation in your life. But remember that the heart of you endures. Your spirit transcends trends, eras, and circumstances. We believe that if you get to the heart of what you love and why you love it, your Style Statement will be true indefinitely, perhaps for a lifetime.

# CONTEMPORARY
# FLOURISH

## Leisa Washington, October 1972

*Charity Coordinator.*

### Contemporary

**SPIRIT:** Contemporary has a strong presence, because they are indeed "present." Contemporary looks you in the eye. They are up-to-date and current with what matters most to them and are typically interested in social and cultural issues. They stay on top of things; they make time work for them; they look to the future. Progressive thinkers, they seek out leading-edge ideas and people to help them get where they want to go. Contemporary is often champion of a cause. They prefer to interact with genuine and authentic people but can tolerate many types of personalities in order to achieve their goals, from having a good time to purpose-driven missions. In overdrive, Contemporary can be forceful or critical, especially of themselves and their healthy limitations. Living from a place of inspiration and always curious, Contemporary turns possibility into real time, with pragmatism, common sense, and a clarity of commitment.

**LOOK & FEEL:** Modern; in style but not necessarily trendy; potentially avant-garde; clean, new, well-cared for. Simple lines; open spaces and surfaces.

### Flourish

*abundant, accomplish, amplify, bloom, blossom, boom, come along, develop, do well, embellish, expand, flow, flower, fruitful, generous, get ahead, get on, giving, glory in, growing, increase, multiply, ornamentation, overflowing, plentiful, plume, prosper, succeed, swell, thrive, triumph*

**CLOCKWISE:** Bath & Body Works lotion (it's all I wear for fragrance), the Bible (I carry it in every purse), African doll, my very first Pumas—they now fit my daughter, duplicate of charm bracelet, event tickets, personalized Roots duffel bag—gives me Leisa Power

**I FEEL MOST AT HOME:** in Jamaica—content, comfortable, humble.

**I ADMIRE:** Oprah. She's smart, brave, helps everyone, and gets what she wants.

**MY DREAM CAREER WOULD BE:** pediatrician. Or a lawyer, to fight for children's rights.

**I'D WEAR TO THE ACADEMY AWARDS:** a very simple, clean-lined dress, not by a well-known designer. A diamond tennis bracelet, strappy sandals.

**I NOURISH MYSELF:** with music—gospel and reggae—and reading the Bible.

**I HAVE A LOT OF:** happiness and wisdom—more than ever before.

**MY PURPOSE IN LIFE:** is to give back, because when I was growing up nobody helped my family and me. I want kids to know that life can get better, so much better.

**IF MONEY WERE NO OBJECT I WOULD:** fly a bunch of inner-city kids and their families to Disney World for a week. I'd buy my sisters cars and bigger homes.

**I FEEL SECURE WHEN:** I have my kids with me, and Gary. When I'm at home. When there's money in the bank.

**MY IDEAL BODY FEELS:** strong and healthy.

**I AM:** a total clean freak.

**ULTIMATE CELEBRATION I'D CREATE:** would be for my mother because she is strong and funny and has been to hell and back. I'd love to take her to Africa for the day.

***CONTEMPORARY* MEANS TO ME:** Humble. Right now. Modern. New. I don't borrow or beg—if I can't buy it, I save for it.

***FLOURISH* MEANS TO ME:** Grow! Prosper! I need people and things that will allow me to flourish and do the good that I want to do. Keep striving. Keep going.

# style, noun

1. The way in which something is said, done, expressed, or performed.

2. A quality of imagination and individuality expressed in one's actions and tastes.

*Handwrites letters with a fountain pen.*

*Dragon tattoo under tailored suit.*

*Collects teapots. Gathers people. Captures ideas.*

*Deeply sensitive. Highly ambitious.*

*Business card: heavy paper stock, embossed, black on white.*

*Tango lessons. Hip-hop. Laid-back.*

*Conservative. Craves order. Country.*

*Fried blonde hair.*

*Matte finish.*

*An old farmhouse on ten acres.*

*Never diamonds. Never imitation. Never late.*

*Wears only silver, only white shirts, only new.*

*Skinny-dips every chance she gets.*

*Vacations in Vegas.*

*Carries Red No. 7 lipstick in every handbag.*

*Hates parties. Loves to be noticed.*

*Saffron robes, black habits, a white sari.*

*Monogrammed cuff links. Family plaid.*

*Mellows out with the Grateful Dead. Prefers Mozart.*

*Big smile. Honest eyes.*

# What Is Style?

It's everything.

Writing style. Speaking style. Leadership style.

Fashion. Art. Architecture. Athletics.

Style is the way you say it, the way you do it, the way you live it.

Sometimes it is an appearance. Sometimes it is an attitude.

Style is the lighting of life. It accentuates, delineates, and conceals.
At its best, style reflects the soul.

### THE STYLE YOU SEE

As sure as we breathe, we style. We've been doing it naturally for millennia, with tribal markings and family plaids, gemstones and silicone implants, mausoleums and urban sprawl. Before there were designer labels, there were coats of arms and portrait painters. Our belongings and adornments announce social rank, the God we worship, and political affiliation. Like the plumage of birds or the patterned wings of a moth, our fashion choices are made to attract a lover, to command attention, or to blend quietly into the background.

History is punctuated with fashion and décor Style Statements. When she cut off her hair and showed up for battle in men's military garb, Joan of Arc made it clear that she would go the distance for her country and her God. They questioned her sanity, but her patriotism was inarguable. The Emperor Shah Jahan styled the ultimate statement of affection for his beloved deceased wife when he built her an exclusive resting place. Twenty-two years in the making, the Taj Mahal is one of the most magnificent symbols of devotion and craftsmanship on Earth.

Fashion can be superficial, but style as an expression of personal truth is never without meaning—in fact, it's the alchemy of the physical plane. Fashion designer Coco Chanel's cultural influence was so strong that she was named in *Time* magazine's list of the one hundred most influential people of the twentieth century—in the company of Winston Churchill and Albert Einstein. Entire industries and generations are defined by their ideas of cool. The top-ten and bestseller lists may seem like flimflam, yet they are anything but.

> The self is our life's goal, for it is the completest expression of that fateful combination we call individuality.
>
> —CARL JUNG

The shape of our creations—from buildings and cars to textiles and neighborhoods—reflect the disposition of the collective psyche.

Style does not hint at what's going on in a culture; it shouts it out with billions of retail dollars, civil movements, and social boundaries. Style is a phenomenal force that is as persuasive as political will and organized religion. It is a currency—of fashion, of technology, of ideologies—that has birthed nations. **Style arouses emotion, triggers deep instincts, and changes people's minds.**

Looking through the rearview mirror, it's easy to spot the big messages in history and pop culture. But look closer, into your own backyard; read between the lines of your life; examine the pattern of your thoughts. **What shape do you take? What is the texture of your mind, the soundtrack of your days? What is your Style Statement?**

### THE STYLE YOU FEEL

**It's not about the fashion; it's about the passion.** Some personas reveal and some conceal. You can be consistently inauthentic and outwardly successful. But the point of defining your own Style Statement is to affirm an identity that reflects the real you. In her book, *The Substance of Style* (New York: HarperCollins, 2003), cultural critic Virginia Postrel sums it up brilliantly: "Identity is the meaning of surface. Sometimes...statements of identity are inadvertent, and occasionally they are false. But in the age of aesthetics, they are inescapable. Effective surfaces, whether for people, places, or things, reveal layers of identity and association while preserving a fundamental sense of self."

### THE STYLE YOU ARE

**Every choice we make is an expression of our beliefs.** On a daily basis, we make material and aesthetic choices that tell our stories. Bold or subtle. Polished or rough. Secluded or central. We compose our identity with sensory messages and symbols. In effect, by conveying ourselves in a particular way, we tell the world how we want to be treated.

We are hardwired toward self-preservation. From the shape of our cells to the swirl of our fingerprints, each human is profoundly, almost incomprehensibly, unique. In all the aeons of time, among the trillions of human eggs that have been fertilized and babies born, **there is only one you**—microscopically remarkable, positively unrepeatable, original, and beyond compare. *That's style.*

GENUINE
LEGACY

# Donald Clifton McMillan III, July 1972

*Engineer. Attorney.*

## Genuine

**SPIRIT:** Authentic and real, Genuine wants to be fully itself and deeply appreciate people and experiences that are free of hypocrisy or dishonesty. Sincerity is sweet music to their souls. They gravitate to those who are down-to-earth and unpretentious. They are expert at sensing the discomfort and needs of others and excel at putting people at ease, drawing on their humor, good manners, or tenderness to do so. Genuine has a knack for taking the best and leaving the rest. They want the facts. They rarely suffer fools, and they don't make much time for situations that go against their grain or distract them from their goals. It's fairly easy for them to walk away from situations that aren't serving them. Genuines' motto tends to be "Live and live." Ironically, Genuine can struggle with balancing its outer image with its inner desires and, for better or worse, will fake it to make it. They have a special fondness for originality and appreciate things that last and endure as well as people and principles that have stood the test of time.

**LOOK & FEEL:** Comfortable and comforting. Strong craftsmanship, standing the test of time. Almost anything goes with Genuines' fashion as long as it feels right. Genuine adores tried-and-true brands and things, and places and people steeped with history and character. Replicas, rip-offs, and imitation designs and materials are out of the question.

## Legacy

*ancestry, background, bequest, birthright, descent, endowment, estate, fabled, famous, gift, heirloom, heritage, heroic, inheritance, legendary, lineage, mythic, nobility, origins, provenance, recognized, stories, supernatural, traditional*

**CLOCKWISE:** Marine Corps Marathon medals, Christ statuette from Rio, my great grandfather's coin that he carried in his pocket during the Depression—even though it was often the only dollar he had; elephant-skin cowboy boots, kilt pin, cuff links, marathon shirt

**MY MOST RIDICULOUS PURCHASE WAS:** first-class tickets to the Virgin Islands and renting a boat for a week to impress a chick—when I couldn't even pay the rent.

**I AM INSPIRED BY:** God!!! When I think of complexity, structure, infinity, and while I watch Her paint a sunset!

**IDEAL CAR:** Aston Martin.

**I CHERISH:** the cross-stitch my sister made for me as a graduation gift.

**I CAN HARDLY TOLERATE:** racism (less than hardly!!!), unforgiving caste systems, title hounds, and surgically altered anything!

**I LOVE:** that the only thing that matters is love and that I had to fall, fail, and flourish to learn that!

**I LOVE THE SMELL OF:** Glacier Lake at 5 a.m., the football field in the fourth quarter, dinner at Grandma's, saltwater spray on my grandfather's boat, the Lost Pines of East Texas.

**WHAT WORKS IN MY WARDROBE:** is my genuine-leather jacket.

**I AM MY BEST SELF WHEN:** I'm told I can't.

**I READ:** *IEEE Spectrum, Business 2.0, The Economist, National Geographic.*

**I WANT MORE:** life, love, memory making, sex, single malts, sunsets, and faith.

**THE LEAKS AND DRAINS IN MY LIFE ARE:** complaints to or from anyone for anything. Taxes!

**MY EVIL TWIN:** is a tree-huggin' virgin who doesn't drink and complains to his congressman about globalization by writing on unrecycled paper with ink tested on animals.

**I FEEL MOST AT HOME:** when I'm committed.

***GENUINE* MEANS TO ME:** Liking who I am and realizing what God gave me is just fine!

***LEGACY* MEANS TO ME:** One day taking my grandson fishing and teaching him about the stars.

When a question is posed ceremoniously, the universe responds.

# Inquire

## Part 2

# WELCOME
# TO THE
# INQUIRY

Here you will visit the eight domains of life via the Lifestyle Map. The questions in each lifestyle section are divided into two categories: "What works well for me" and "What does not work well for me." Becoming aware of this kind of contrast is an effective way to clarify what you value most.

You will be asked to look beneath the surface of your life. You will be asked to wonder, to remember, and to feel. You will be encouraged to dream big. **You will be guided to make connections and draw your own conclusions.** In this way, meaning and themes will start to emerge, and new insights might pop into your mind. This process is all about pattern recognition.

Some questions are intimate and expansive; others are playful and seemingly trivial. But each answer will reveal a thin slice of your core. Remember, you do not have to answer every question, nor is it necessary to follow the sequence of sections or questions in this book. Follow your own rhythm.

Some questions may make you uncomfortable and uneasy, or you may feel like you're staring at a blank wall. Don't panic. Move on, then come back to the question. Call a friend and talk it out. You both may be invigorated by this investigation.

We also encourage you to make up your own questions. For inspiration, read through the Style Statement profiles in this book. You'll find some unique questions that are not included in the inquiry exercises that follow.

When you're answering questions in the "What works well for me" section, be thinking: *I am attracted to…I am inspired by…This feels right to me…I am compelled by…I feel desire for…I feel satisfied by…*

When you're answering questions in the "What does not work well for me" section, be thinking: *I am repelled by…I dislike…This doesn't feel right…I have no patience for…I feel dissatisfied…I experience displeasure…*

At the end of each section, there is a space for you to **sift through the key words and ideas from your answers.** This filtered-out collection of words and thoughts are clues to your Style Statement.

# Style Stretch: An Inquiry

Style Statements, along with sweet longings and life callings, are rooted in your subconscious. So it's time to warm up your introspective muscles and stretch out your creative bones.

Remember, there is no right or wrong answer. If you're torn between choices, either force yourself to choose (sometimes pushing yourself to make a decision offers valuable insights in these types of exercises) or skip it and go back to it later.

**ASK YOURSELF *WHY?***
When you have completed the exercise, scan your choices and ask yourself this profoundly important question: *why?*

Why do you relate to *planner* vs. *impulsive?* Because it seems professional and responsible to you? Because you have a fear of the unknown? Because your mother disapproves of impulsiveness?

Why milk chocolate over dark chocolate? Because milk chocolate reminds you of sweet childhood memories? Because dark chocolate is bitter and too grown-up? Because it's all you've ever tried?

You don't have to record your answers, and you certainly don't have to ask why about every set of words. But if you can, start to put thoughts, words, and reasons to your preferences. Knowing why you're attracted to or inspired by or prefer something is the golden key to opening up your Style Statement possibilities.

READ EACH WORD PAIR, THEN CIRCLE THE WORD THAT YOU FEEL THE MOST CONNECTION WITH. TRY NOT TO OVERTHINK YOUR CHOICES. MAKE YOUR SELECTIONS FROM THE HEART. IMPULSIVENESS CAN BE ENERGIZING.

| | | |
|---|---|---|
| Introvert / Extrovert | Leather / Lace | History / Pop culture |
| Matte / Glossy | New York / LA | Diamonds / Emeralds |
| Cabin / Condo | Oprah / Martha | Direct / Subtle |
| Handwritten / Typed | Poetry / Gospel | Plaid / Stripes |
| Off-white / Gray | Rustic / Retro | Fur / Hemp |
| Silver / Gold | Coffee / Tea | Fiction / Nonfiction |
| Round / Square | Educated / Street-smart | Tulips / Roses |
| Fight / Flight | Streamlined / Overstuffed | Digital / Analog |
| Jazz / Classical | Cotton / Raw silk | Astrology / Astronomy |
| Answer the phone / Voicemail | Crystal / Carvings | Soccer / Baseball |
| Frugal / Spendy | Medication / Meditation | Politics / Philosophy |
| Indoor / Outdoor | Follower / Leader | Picasso / Monet |
| Heritage / Contemporary | Rebel / Peacemaker | Sexy / Ladylike |
| Anxious / Chilled | Clutter / Sparse | Piles / Files |
| Liberal / Conservative | Tofu / Steak | Impulsive / Planner |
| Red wine / White wine | Day timer / Memory | Lone ranger / Team player |
| Trusting / Cautious | Chrome / Copper | Smooth / Rough |
| Gregarious / Shy | Naked / Pajamas | Handshake / Hug |
| Milk chocolate / Dark chocolate | Moody / Bubbly | Sweet / Sour |
| Live theater / New DVD | Pencil / Pen | Warrior / Magician |
| Morning person / Night owl | Nightly News / MTV | Romantic / Realistic |

# Style Run: An Inquiry

WHAT ARE YOU SENSITIVE TO?

WHAT ARE YOU MOST GRATEFUL FOR?

WHAT DO YOU LIKE TO BE NOTICED FOR?

HOW DO YOU DEAL WITH BEING RUSHED?

WHEN HAVE YOU BEEN UNEXPECTEDLY STRONG?

WHEN HAVE YOU BEEN UNEXPECTEDLY VULNERABLE?

WHAT KIND OF SHOES ARE YOU DRAWN TO?




HOW DO YOU FEEL ABOUT SHOPPING?




HOW DO YOU FEEL IN A BOOKSTORE?




WHAT DOES YOUR VOICE SOUND LIKE TO YOU?




WHAT ARE SOME OF YOUR FAVORITE WORDS?




WHAT WOULD YOU LIKE TO REVOLUTIONIZE?

# SIMPLY
## CRAFTED

**CLOCKWISE:** Garden bucket, Felco pruners, Blundstone boots, my son's jam, Grandmother's knitting needle pouch, *Appetite* by Nigel Slater, *The Bread Baker's Apprentice* by Peter Reinhart and Ron Manville, *Homegrown* by Michel Nischan, *The Anatomy of a Dish* by Diane Forley and Catherine Young, *A Blessing of Bread* by Maggie Glezer, toys that I knit—"Grit & Grace"

**THINGS I LOVE:** That my son leans toward happiness, that my daughter only asks quirky questions; planning the vegetable garden in January; tea and cheese scones with good friends.

**BOOKS THAT HAVE DEFINED ME:** *Pride and Prejudice* by Jane Austen, *The Complete Shakespeare* by Pelican Publishers, *Appetite* by Nigel Slater, *The Best Recipes* by Cook's Illustrated, *Home Cooking* by Laurie Colwin, *The Blessing of a Skinned Knee* by Wendy Mogel.

**I AM INTERESTED IN:** getting to the core. Preserving the unique and individual. Slowing down the speed at which my family lives. Making as much as possible from scratch. Midcentury ranchers.

**MY JEWELRY:** Don't wear any. I'm not into adornment.

**MY FAVORITE FLOWER:** Sweet pea. So honest and basic and lovely. And I have a thing for the euphorbia bush.

**I AM MY BEST SELF:** early in the morning.

**I COLLECT:** information. Dishes from Hycroft China. Tweed yarn. Children's stories.

**I CRAVE:** dark chocolate with no bitter aftertaste.

**MY TRIBE IS:** earthbound.

**I AM IMPRESSED BY PEOPLE WHO:** are honest with themselves.

**YOU COULDN'T PAY ME ENOUGH TO:** eat trans fats.

**ARTISTIC WORKS THAT INSPIRE ME:** The Hundertwasser House in Vienna, pretty much any knit designed by Kaffe Fassett, and the ranch home by Cliff May.

**MY FAVORITE FORM OF PLAY IS:** hiking in Palm Springs, particularly up Smoke Tree Mountain along Garstin Trail.

**YOU'D NEVER CATCH ME WEARING:** someone else's logo. I prefer to make my clothes.

**IF I WERE BORN INTO A DIFFERENT CULTURE:** I'm stuck here for now.

***SIMPLY* MEANS TO ME:** capturing the essence of somebody or something in a way that is easy, a way that flows, a way that is true.

***CRAFTED* MEANS TO ME:** capturing the essence of somebody or something in a way that is easy, a way that flows, a way that is true.

# The Spirit and Look & Feel of your life…

| | | |
|---|---|---|
| **Home**<br>Dwelling space.<br>+<br>**Stuff**<br>What you own, collect, desire. | **Fashion**<br>Clothing. Adornment.<br>+<br>**Sensuality**<br>5 Senses. Sexuality. | **Spirit**<br>Divine life. Inspiration.<br>+<br>**Learning**<br>Seeking experience and knowledge. |
| **Service**<br>Work. Philanthropy.<br>+<br>**Wealth**<br>Income. Outflow. | **You** | **Relationships**<br>Friends. Romance. Family. Colleagues.<br>+<br>**Communication**<br>Tools for interacting. |
| **Creativity**<br>Ideas. Creations.<br>+<br>**Celebration**<br>Occasions. Gifts. | **Body**<br>Food. Exercise.<br>+<br>**Wellness**<br>Care and healing. | **Nature**<br>The elements.<br>+<br>**Rest & Relaxation**<br>What calms and entertains you. |

## STRUCTURED MAGIC

Kim Christie,
*Photographer*

I love being an adult. I love that I can do whatever I want, whenever I want. It just feels great to be in charge—the absolute freedom of it. What I possess, in spades, is effusive, eccentric, wild-card energy.

Before my Style Statement, I would have said that my artistic nature was my greatest attribute. But my Style Statement is Structured Magic. And it really made me step back and realize that the shazam and pizzazz rests on solid grid lines. And if I forget that, I can definitely feel myself floating off into the ether. It's evident everywhere in my life. My living room is a pop-art display of orange and red, but that only works because the hard landscape of architecture and furniture is absolute symmetry, perpendicular lines, bisecting angles—solid and steady and mathematically correct. And for me to jazz with energy and ideas, everything—from my day planner to my diet to my exercise and meditation regime—has to be structured. The structure is what supports the magic. It is, in fact, what feeds it.

## TIMELESS ALLURE

Brenda McAllister,
*Service Specialist*

Now I understand my last-minute dash back to my closet to throw that rhinestone belt around my neck. I understand my attraction to the really big candelabras and my need to envelop my house with love and warmth. I understand why it is so important that my family, friends, and guests feel like they are the most important people in the world when they are with me. I understand why I have to turn the music up to dance on the table and encourage everyone around me to do the same. I understand why I bought my daughter a hot-pink bike with leopard print and encouraged my son to paint his bike to suit himself. It's all about being yourself—the real you.

My Style Statement gives me permission to be myself. It also makes me responsible to be my true self. I can't imagine living any other way.

## TRADITIONAL FEMININE

Michelle Pante,
*Business Adviser*

I have a BA in sociology, a BSW, an MBA, and I strongly identify as a feminist. So Traditional Feminine was not an obvious match for me. I used to feel confused when I was drawn to traditional things and ways of being (like my delicate, princess-cut wedding ring and my yearning to be a full-time mom) because I perceived myself as so independent and modern.

But the truth is clear within my directions and desires. I chose to study *both* social work and business; to return to the Catholic Church after years away; to name our child in honor of family members. I love to feed friends. I adore family legacy and ritual. Since my Style Statement "realization," I'm celebrating my feminine power in ways that are more truly and naturally me. And *that* is liberation!

## SOPHISTICATED FRESH

### Tanya Schoenroth,
*Interior Designer*

I aim to approach all situations with a grace and integrity true to the values I associate with my Style Statement. As a self-employed designer, projecting confidence in my decisions is integral to my ability to communicate with and gain the trust and respect of my clients. Previously, I put too much emphasis on the Fresh side of my personality, because I so wanted everyone to like me. I imagine the effect was that I was interpreted as being a bit too chipper and perhaps not serious about my work. For me, changing the focus to Sophisticated meant quieting my insecurities, and the part of my brain that suspected opinions contrary to my own were automatically more valid. While I am flexible and open to the suggestions of others, I've learned that part of my service is having a strong opinion on design direction, as well as evidence to back it up.

Sophisticated Fresh has added an air of maturity to my communication. I'm not sure that others can discern a difference, but the end result is that I am increasingly centered and precise in my work and life.

## GRACEFUL INVITATION

### Catherine Diamond,
*Charity Coordinator*

I am starting to invite myself into life. I must admit, trying new things is sometimes scary. I have invited myself to achieve my goal of health and wellness. I feel more deserving, and putting myself first makes me feel more graceful, my true self.

My husband has observed a calmer Catherine, and this has strengthened our relationship. I am slowly, sometimes with trepidation, stating what pleases me, inviting his help, asking him to massage my feet, my back; inviting him to sit with me on the couch; asking for what makes me happy. He's thrilled that I am inviting him in! I had forgotten what a wonderful man I had married! I find that instead of saying something critical, I try to find something positive amid the negative, the confusion, and the sadness life can bring. It sure makes for a far lovelier life and marriage. I feel that my authentic self is emerging at the age of fifty-four—clearly never too late! Graceful Invitation will be a lifelong journey for me.

## TRADITIONAL CURRENT

### Lucia Frangione,
*Actress*

In my career as a writer and an actor, I am drawn to themes of family, examining the virtues of cultural ideologies and core religious beliefs, yet I write from a feminist perspective and love to play with innovative form. Who the heck am I? What world do I live in? Do I have to give up one or the other?

Having my Style Statement gives me great peace and a sort of validation. It's OK to be 80% Traditional and 20% Current. In fact, it's fabulous! The most important things to me are family, my Christian beliefs, history, and art. I don't have to apologize for that. Somebody has to keep tradition going! And yet, I don't need to stay "stuck" in tradition. I can honor it, love it, immerse myself in it, and yet bring a 20% wahoo, I'm gonna turn you on your ear now sort of energy to it. I suppose it's the responsibility of Traditional Current to breathe new life into old classics. So I wear my Sofia Loren dress with quirky, hip shoes; I cook dinner for my macho husband who loves that I'm a successful artist; I write my Jesus erotica and phone my nonna on Sundays. Life is 100% wonderful.

# COMFORTABLE PURITY

Cameron Thorn,
*Real Estate Developer*

 501 Levis on the weekend and Paul Smith suits during the week, that's me. Connecting with people over great conversation, organic food and great wine is me. Kayaking in Desolation Sound on the British Columbia coast with my buddies comforts my soul, and blue Pilot pens lined up on my desk feeds my desire for order.

The island house we are building will be simple in design and support my commitment to green living. We shall create a space that is inviting where I can feel at home and create comfort and ease for our friends and family. My struggle is to maintain that ease during the work week.

I know when my attention to detail gets in the way because my wife gently nudges me to have more stillness in my life. My Style Statement Comfortable Purity supports me in my pursuit of balance and drive.

# SIMPLISTIC EARTH

Scott Johnson,
*Firefighter*

 I have defined myself experiencing canoe trips, mountain climbing, tree planting, and plunging into frozen rivers from makeshift sweat lodges. The wilderness is a spiritual celebration for me. There is nothing like a river to remind me of my place in the world.

But at some point along the way, I started to spend more time working and less time playing and feeding my soul. Exploring gave way to achieving. I'm very goal oriented but sometimes, goals can distract you from the other things in life that matter most.

I say what I mean, and I prefer to take the most direct route from problems to solutions—simple and true. I admire honest, hearty characters and eccentric perspectives. I'm building a life based on respect, hard work, and fun—the down-to-earth kind of fun. My wife, my son, my dog—home is central to me.

So Simplistic Earth reminds me what matters most: deepening my roots, growing my family, keeping it natural, and finding new mountains to climb.

# CONSTRUCTED
# PLAYFUL

# DEFINITION

Klee Larsen, April 1986

*Photographer.*

## Constructive

**SPIRIT:** Constructive love rhythm, order, patterns, circuitry, cohesiveness, fine-tuning, and all roads that lead to harmony. They are a wonderful combination of pragmatism and warmth. They love the interplay of experiences and qualities and memories that build on each other to form relationships. Making things happen, creating results, and being clearly expressive are all core motivators for Constructive. Whether it's an improved system, a work of art, or a dinner party, Constructive must keep things moving in the right direction—and usually have a precise way of getting there. They need a sound foundation of love or ritual in their lives, or a sense of disconnectedness or worry can creep in. Support systems are key to their well-being and productivity. Constructive can be a forgiving friend or partner and are of strong and generous character, always facing up to life and making the most of what they have to work with.

**LOOK & FEEL:** Sturdy, complex, detailed, strategic, systematic; rhythmical beats, patterns, graphics; strong shapes, bold colors; highly contoured, architectural, tailored elements; socially responsible manufacturing and production.

## Playful

*adventuresome, amusing, artful, cheerful, clever, coy, creative, entertaining, fanciful, good-natured, happy, humorous, ironic, irreverent, joyous, lighthearted, lively, mischievous, recreating, relaxing, satirical, saucy, smart, spirited, vivacious, whimsical, witty*

**CLOCKWISE:** Skateboard (a gift from ex-boyfriend), fedora from my collection, old pottery jar lid, antlers, figure skateblade, art from high school art class, plaster foot made by Janaki, light-up globe, enamel glazing powder

**I LOVE:** raw, imperfect leather. Simple shapes and burst of color. Cathedrals! The details are amazing. Tom Waits. Hanging with my friends. White beach bungalows.

**IF I LIVED IN A DIFFERENT ERA:** I'd be totally self-indulgent, Marie Antoinette–style.

**I WANT MORE THAN ANYTHING:** A Hasselblad camera with a digital backing.

**I AM INSPIRED BY ART THAT:** takes me longer than two seconds to look at. I love the work of Andy Goldsworthy—it doesn't last, but he's still doing it. I love the impermanence.

**I WANT MY WARDROBE TO FEEL:** more classic, with more basic and fundamental things.

**IF MONEY WERE NO OBJECT:** I'd buy a plane ticket around the world, today!

**I LOVE MOST ABOUT MYSELF:** My spontaneity.

**I AM MY BEST SELF WHEN:** I've had ten hours of sleep and a cup of coffee.

**IF IT WERE MORE SOCIALLY ACCEPTABLE, I WOULD:** skinny-dip all the time.

**MY TATTOOS ARE:** a white circle on my back and one on my ankle. My next tattoo is going to be a white sparrow on my forearm, because sparrows are free to do whatever they want to do.

**I AM REPELLED BY:** belittling.

**I AM FASCINATED BY:** phosphorescences.

**I'M SCARED OF:** being in debt.

**MY FRIENDS WOULD SAY:** that I love to laugh and to make things. And that you never know what's going to come out of my mouth.

***CONSTRUCTIVE* MEANS TO ME:** Being able to put things together. Coming up with ideas; problem solving.

***PLAYFUL* MEANS TO ME:** Being a kid and seeing the world. Having fun with everyday things.

## Home
**Dwelling space.**

**+**

## Stuff
**What you own, collect, desire.**

*Born and raised.*

*Driving fast.*

*Surfing waves. Surfing the Web.*

*It all happens in my kitchen.*

*White peonies are proud but gentle.*

*Rows and rows. Piles on top of piles.*

*Small town anywhere.*

*In the arms of her lover.*

*Priceless.*

*Secluded but convenient.*

*Sunday service.*

*The cosmos.*

*In cashmere.*

*Jack's Pub, 5 p.m.*

*Junkyard.*

*Crystal. Silver. China.*

*Heritage.*

*On the Harley, with the wind in his hair.*

*Completely at ease.*

# What Works Well for Me

**I FEEL MOST AT HOME:**

*This is the place where you feel most grounded and connected to yourself.*

**HOW DO YOU FEEL WHEN YOU'RE THERE?**

*What does it bring out in you? What do other people associate with this place? What is this kind of place most known for?*

**WHAT I VALUE MOST ABOUT THE PLACE (THE SPACE AND THE COMMUNITY) IN WHICH I LIVE IS:**

**A FEW OBJECTS IN MY LIVING SPACE THAT I CHERISH OR TAKE GREAT PLEASURE IN:**

*What do you like so much about each piece/place? What's its style? Its era? Its origin? What's the story behind it?*

**MY DREAM HOME IS:**

*What is the architectural style? How would your interests and essence be reflected? What kind of artwork would you bring in?*

**IF I COULD HAVE BEEN BORN INTO A DIFFERENT CULTURE OR TIME PERIOD, IT WOULD HAVE BEEN:**

*What feels attractive to you about that place or era? What would you most appreciate or delight in?*

**I LONG TO TRAVEL TO AND/OR ONE OF MY FAVORITE PLACES TO VISIT IS:**

*What about that place that is calling to you? What do you love most about that area or culture?*

**MY PERSONAL SANCTUARY IS:**

**I AM AT EASE THERE BECAUSE IT IS:**

**A COMPLETELY LUXURIOUS, OUTRAGEOUS THING THAT I'D LIKE TO OWN IS:**

**BECAUSE:**

**I COLLECT OR HAVE A LOT OF:**

*What appeals to you about these things? What do they represent to you? What is special or meaningful about them?*

# Filter & Interpret your answers

What words or concepts **feel important or intriguing** to you?

What **themes** are showing up in your answers?

What **words, images, or feelings** are crossing your mind?

# What Does *Not* Work Well for Me

**I HAVE FELT OUT OF PLACE OR INCREDIBLY UNCOMFORTABLE:**

*Describe what that time or place looks like, feels like, sounds like. How do you feel when you're there?*

**SOME THINGS IN MY LIVING SPACE THAT I WANT TO TOSS BUT HAVEN'T OR CAN'T:**

*What do you dislike about them?*

**THE MOST RIDICULOUS PURCHASE I EVER MADE WAS:**

**BECAUSE:**

**MY IDEA OF AN UNAPPEALING LIVING PLACE OR CULTURE IS:**

*Describe why that environment is unsuited to you or what feels most out of line with your needs and likes.*

**IF SOMEONE DIDN'T KNOW ME VERY WELL, THEY'D TAKE ME ON A DATE TO:**

**IT WOULD BE DISASTROUS BECAUSE:**

# Filter & Interpret your answers

What words or concepts **feel important or intriguing** to you?

What **themes** are showing up in your answers?

What **words, images, or feelings** are crossing your mind?

# GENUINE
# ELEGANCE

# Audrey Beaulac, October 1959

*Image and Style Consultant.*

## Genuine

**SPIRIT:** Authentic and real, Genuine wants to be fully itself and deeply appreciate people and experiences that are free of hypocrisy or dishonesty. Sincerity is sweet music to their souls. They gravitate to those who are down-to-earth and unpretentious. They are expert at sensing the discomfort and needs of others and so excel at putting people at ease, drawing on their humor, good manners, or tenderness to do so. Genuine has a knack for taking the best and leaving the rest. They want the facts. They rarely suffer fools, and they don't make much time for situations that go against their grain or distract them from their goals. It's fairly easy for them to walk away from situations that aren't serving them. Genuine's motto tends to be "Live and live." Ironically, Genuine can struggle with balancing its outer image with its inner desires and, for better or worse, will fake it to make it. They have a special fondness for originality and appreciate things that last and endure as well as people and principles that have stood the test of time.

**LOOK & FEEL:** Comfortable and comforting. Strong craftsmanship, standing the test of time. Almost anything goes with Genuine's fashion as long as it feels right. Genuine adores tried-and-true brands and things, and places and people steeped with history and character. Replicas, rip-offs, and imitation designs and materials are out of the question.

## Elegance

*appropriate, apt, artistic, balance, beauty, charm, clarity, choice, class, classic, cultivation, culture, delicacy, dignity, discernment, distinction, effective, exquisiteness, gentility, good, grace, grandeur, ingenious, lushness, luxury, magnificence, ornateness, polish, purity, refinement, restraint, rhythm, simplicity, sophistication, splendor, stylized, sumptuousness, symmetry, taste, tastefulness*

**CLOCKWISE:** Photograph, a candle shaped like a thread cone (from Barcelona), stylized dressmaker's bust, glass egg (one of my favorite color combinations), crystals from my mother, dish from North Virginia

**WHEN I WAS YOUNG, I DREAMED OF BECOMING:** a jet-setter.

**MY FAVORITE FLOWER IS:** the Casablanca lily. I love the clean soft white contrasted with the dark, rich green leaves and stem. The fragrance is intoxicating; it makes me think of tropical islands.

**MY DEFINITION OF BEAUTY:** A harmonious coordination in any form that enhances me physically and spiritually.

**I READ:** books on business development, evolution of the human spirit, and spirituality, as well as *WWD,* fashion magazines, all major department store catalogs, trend reports, and school newsletters.

**I'D WEAR TO THE ACADEMY AWARDS:** An evening suit in squid ink green, with a fabulous Renee Bassetti custom shirt, cuffs turned down to my knuckles. An extraordinary shoe, gorgeous Miriam Haskell earrings, full hair, clean makeup, with perfect eyebrows and lips.

**WOMEN WHOSE LOOK I ADMIRE:** Slim Keith, Katharine Hepburn, Judy Davis. As for designers, I'm infatuated with Fortuny, Balenciaga, and Oscar de la Renta right now.

**THE BEST MATERIAL GIFT I'VE RECEIVED WAS:** a photo album my husband made and a poem he wrote for our first anniversary.

**I LOVE TEXTILES THAT:** have weight. I'm currently drawn to double-faced wool and sensual, luscious Irish linens.

**MY BELIEF SYSTEM:** To live in service to other people, to seek harmony with universal principles.

**MY FORM OF EXERCISE:** Swimming—almost daily.

**MY FORM OF GENIUS:** is color. Everybody has a unique palette that belongs to them; I have a gift for seeing an individual's colors accurately and reflecting them back in a meaningful way.

**ONE OUTFIT FOR THE REST OF MY LIFE:** Jeans, a T-shirt, bare feet, my Parisian earrings, and seven gold rings.

**WHEN I'M INSPIRED:** I design my life and buy books on Amazon. I've got a lot of books.

***GENUINE* MEANS TO ME:** Authenticity—striving to define your own style and live it.

***ELEGANCE* MEANS TO ME:** Prioritizing aesthetic practices and seamless service.

## Fashion
**Clothing. Adornment.**

**+**

## Sensuality
**5 Senses. Sexuality.**

*Naked.*

*Prestige.*

*Consignment store.*

*Erotica.*

*Homemade.*

*My morning ritual.*

*Overthought. Impulse purchase. Second nature.*

*Cultured pearls. Stacked bangles.*

*Power suit. Wet suit. Well suited.*

*Lingering scent.*

*Black because it hides. Black for devotion.*

*Neutral. Simple. Ease.*

*Only on special occasions.*

*Secretly pierced.*

*Barely there.*

*Leather with lace.*

*Wash 'n' go mommy.*

*Sweet 'n' savory.*

*Handle with care.*

# What Works Well for Me

**WHAT'S WORKING IN MY WARDROBE RIGHT NOW IS:**

*What are some pieces that you really love and why? How do you feel when you wear those pieces?*

**AS FOR CELEBRITIES AND PEOPLE I KNOW, THE LOOK THAT I REALLY RESONATE WITH IS:**

**THEIR REPUTATION OR CLASSIFICATION MIGHT BE CALLED:**

**IF I COULD ONLY WEAR ONE OUTFIT FOR THE REST OF MY LIFE, IT WOULD BE:**

*This is not about being practical or appropriate or in style. You could choose stiletto heels, a sari, or a tuxedo. What outfit would make you feel fabulous and truly you? How would you describe this outfit? How do you think others would describe it?*

**I LOOKED MOST FABULOUS:**

*This can be a time in your life or an event. Describe how you looked and felt.*

**THE KIND OF JEWELRY OR FLOURISH I PREFER TO WEAR IS:**

*Describe the style of your accessories and why you prefer them.*

EVEN THOUGH IT'S COMPLETELY OUT OF STYLE OR OVER THE TOP, I SECRETLY LOVE:

BECAUSE:

WHAT I WOULD LOVE TO HAVE MADE FOR ME IS:

MY DEFINITION OF SEXY:

MY FAVORITE FABRICS, TEXTILES, TEXTURES:

BECAUSE:

IN TERMS OF SCENTS AND FRAGRANCES, I AM MOST ATTRACTED TO:

BECAUSE IT MAKES ME FEEL: OR REMINDS ME OF:

IF MONEY WERE NO OBJECT I WOULD GO OUT TODAY AND SHOP FOR:

*Be specific.*

# Filter & Interpret your answers

What words or concepts **feel important or intriguing** to you?

What **themes** are showing up in your answers?

What **words, images, or feelings** are crossing your mind?

# What Does *Not* Work Well for Me

WHAT'S NOT WORKING ABOUT MY WARDROBE IS:

WHEN I WEAR SOMETHING THAT ISN'T REALLY "ME," I FEEL:

SOME OF MY "WHAT WAS I THINKING?" PURCHASES HAVE BEEN:

I FEEL OUT OF TOUCH WITH MY SENSE OF:

YOU'D NEVER CATCH ME WEARING:

BECAUSE:

# Filter & Interpret your answers

What words or concepts **feel important or intriguing** to you?

What **themes** are showing up in your answers?

What **words, images, or feelings** are crossing your mind?

CURRENT
SENSUAL

## Navjit Kandola, July 1968

*Minister. Teacher. Filmmaker.*

### Current

**SPIRIT:** Current is intensely energetic, electrical, moving, and steadily flowing, and often acts as a channel or conductor for multidimensional energy. Their hearts' desire is to connect with the divine and to bring that radiance forward to enhance and enliven others. Artistically and creatively gifted, they very naturally find a way to express their deepest nature and desires. They thrive on exchanges of ideas and concepts and on interactions in commerce or with other people. They are incredibly engaging, often generous to a fault, and talkative. They love to be the center of attention and are at ease with admirers and adulation. They often seem to have an endless supply of energy. In excess, Current can become zealous or righteous and have a tendency to over-spiritualize or over-intellectualize. Always moving forward, Current is a progressive, modern thinker, liberal to proudly radical, up-to-date and topical in their views and opinions.

**LOOK & FEEL:** Modern, contemporary, new, in fashion, hip, avant-garde. Currents are health and eco-conscious and aspire to purity. Organic, uninterrupted clean lines, simplified, vibrant, well-lit. Relevant and essential, pared down.

### Sensual

*arousing, atmosphere, aura, awareness, bodily, capacity, clearheadedness, consciousnesses, delight, discernment, dreamy, epicurean, erotic, feeling, fleshly, gourmet, imagination, insight, intelligence, intuition, judgment, knowledge, luxury-loving, libertine, loving, lush, perception, pleasure, reasoning, relaxation, relish, sensitivity, sentiment, sight, soul, spirit, tactile, taste, understanding, wisdom*

**CLOCKWISE:** Vitamins, blue-green algae drink (full of amino acids!), hand statue (the mudra being gestured here is "Fear Not"), shell from North Carolina coast, mango, light! (It makes my heart and soul bouncy—it is the oldest part of us.)

**I LOVE:** the symmetry and cycles of plants and flowers; all living things because there is something so honest to them; puppies; lightning. I love great books that make you remember that there are brilliant thinkers on the planet, showing choices that say yes to life. I love an audience. I love to witness grace and magnanimity in people, nobility of spirit. I love great shoes.

**I WANT TO TRAVEL:** on an archaeological hunt in the Gobi Desert.

**PHILOSOPHY ON MONEY:** You can't take it personally. It comes and goes. Live your life.

**ONE OUTFIT FOR THE REST OF MY LIFE:** A bikini.

**I FIND SEXY:** Humor, hands, nakedness in all ways.

**MY PHILOSOPHY ON FRIENDSHIP:** Engage with abandon. Give your friends every chance you can.

**TOOLS OF MY TRADE:** Light, nutrition, consciousness, humor, intuition, generosity of spirit.

**MY INNER RHYTHM:** is under the radar.

**FAVORITE FLOWER:** Poppies. Their petals are like butterflies.

**OBJECTS I CHERISH:** Nothing at all, really.

**I WOULD LIKE TO REVOLUTIONIZE:** our relationship to light, emotions, and the concept of ownership.

**I NOURISH MY WELL-BEING:** with yoga, Pilates, laughing, superfoods like sun chlorella, super blue-green algae, CQ10, and colostrum.

**I FEEL UNCOMFORTABLE:** in business attire.

**A COMPLETELY OUTRAGEOUS THING I'D LIKE TO OWN:** A ranch where horses run free.

**BOOKS THAT CHANGED MY LIFE:** *Ecstasy Is a New Frequency* by Chris Griscom, *A Brief History of Everything* by Ken Wilber, *Dune* by Frank Herbert.

***CURRENT* MEANS TO ME:** Motion, not stagnant; finding the best way to get from point A to point B. A lightning-like intelligence.

***SENSUAL* MEANS TO ME:** The best of being in body. Delicious, juicy, rich, fantastic joy.

Spirit
Divine life. Inspiration.
+
Learning
Seeking experience
and knowledge.

*Living the questions.*
*Character. Code. Conduct.*
*To hear with my body. To see with my heart.*
*PhD. Street-smart.*
*Proverbs 16:24.*
*Systems. Logic. Comfortable with risk.*
*Rapture. Samadhi. Bliss.*
*Fractals. Chaos theory. Möbius strip.*
*Time is an illusion.*
*Atheist and sticking to it.*
*Burning in the center of your heart.*
*Scripture. Sutras. Love notes.*
*Mind over matter.*
*Capricorn. Conservative. Cosmology.*
*Photographic memory.*
*All quadrants. All levels.*
*Heavenly. Galactic.*
*Agent of change.*
*God. Goddess.*
*Burned ashes and marigolds.*
*The center of the universe.*

# What Works Well for Me

**THINGS I LOVE:**
*(Stuff, places, ideas, concepts. Be sure to include the reasons why these things appeal to you or have value to you.)*

**I NOURISH MY WELL-BEING BY:**

**WHAT I LOVE MOST ABOUT MYSELF IS:**

**WHAT I'D LIKE MORE OF IN MY LIFE IS:**
*(If you'd like more time or money, describe what you'd do with more time or money.)*

**IF I HAD MORE OF THAT I'D FEEL:**

**I AM MY BEST SELF WHEN:**
**AND MY BEST SELF IS FULLY:**

IF I COULD BECOME A MASTER OR AFICIONADO OF ANYTHING, I WOULD I LIKE TO KNOW THE MOST ABOUT:

BECAUSE THAT AREA IS SO:

I FEEL SECURE WHEN:

MY DEFINITION OF BEAUTY IS:

I FIND MYSELF MOST CONSISTENTLY LONGING FOR:

A TINY PART OF ME SECRETLY WANTS:

# Filter & Interpret your answers

What words or concepts **feel important or intriguing** to you?

What **themes** are showing up in your answers?

What **words, images, or feelings** are crossing your mind?

# What Does *Not* Work Well for Me

THE SELF-CRITICAL STORY THAT I TELL MYSELF MOST OFTEN IS THAT:

WHAT I WANT LESS OF IN MY LIFE IS:

THE LESSON IN MY LIFE THAT KEEPS REPEATING IS:

THE NEGATIVE QUALITIES IN PEOPLE THAT I CAN HARDLY TOLERATE ARE:

MY EVIL TWIN IS:

I'M AFRAID OF:

# Filter & Interpret your answers

What words or concepts **feel important or intriguing** to you?

What **themes** are showing up in your answers?

What **words, images, or feelings** are crossing your mind?

INNOVATIVE
FEMININE

## Melody Biringer, July 1962

*Entrepreness.*

### Innovative

**SPIRIT:** Consummate entrepreneurs, Innovative is always on the lookout for the next big thing, a breakthrough idea, or an invention. Innovative is forever seeking ways to renew, recharge, and replenish, and has a hard time with stagnation and unyieldingness. Perceptive, in tune, and extraordinarily resourceful, Innovative has a knack for finding and creating opportunities that lead to prosperity in multiple ways. They are connectors, mavens, and enthusiastic and natural networkers who make things happen. But Innovative has a tendency to rush ahead or be dismissive of thoughts and experiences before they have been thoroughly explored. And with so many ideas to pursue, they can take on too much. They have a fascination with eccentric people and certainly have a few of their own quirks and eccentricities. They are unabashedly insatiable and determined. Fabulous cheerleaders and champions, Innovative adores being adored and blossoms with acknowledgement and adulation.

**LOOK & FEEL:** Unique, individualized, avant-garde, creative, cutting edge. Can range from high concept and highly stylized to quirky and whimsical. Custom-made and tailored. Typically simple and streamlined.

### Feminine

*changeable, charming, compassionate, creative, curvy, delicate, effeminate, fair, fertile, gentle, girlish, goddess, graceful, intuitive, knowing, ladylike, mama, nurturing, powerful, pure, refined, seductive, sensitive, sexy, shy, soft, tender, womanly*

**CLOCKWISE:** Marshmallows; card from a friend; white shirt; Jaguar— my favorite car; the best time of year is strawberry season; *Crave* books: Vancouver, Seattle, San Francisco—the urban girl's manifesto and best places to do business in these cities

**I LOVE:** new ideas, starting up businesses. White lofts, white shirts, white leather couches. Jaguar cars. Marshmallows. My Sony Vaio laptop and my iPod. Amsterdam.

**I AM INSPIRED:** by working with women—the energy, camaraderie, friendship, and flow of ideas—it constantly moves me forward.

**MY WARDROBE:** is full of white, black, and gray, with the random pink thrown in.

**MY FORM OF GENIUS:** is negotiating. Schmoozing. Relationships.

**THE TOOL OF MY TRADE:** My "I can do anything" attitude.

**I'M MY BEST SELF:** when I am walking and talking.

**I'M SCARED OF:** not a whole lot.

**I LOATHE:** deprivation.

**THE BEST GIFT I'VE GIVEN:** Mentorship.

**UNINTERESTED IN OR BORED BY:** People who talk and don't do.

**I CRAVE:** quality time with my husband, massages, time with girlfriends, traveling, and sugar!

**THE LESSON IN MY LIFE THAT KEEPS REPEATING IS:** finding a positive outcome to any situation.

**MY PHILOSOPHY ON MONEY:** Spend it after you make it.

**I AM VERY INTRIGUED:** by great design.

**I WANT LESS:** of the impulse to interrupt my husband. It drives him crazy.

***INNOVATIVE* MEANS TO ME:** Fresh ideas with swizzle twists.

***FEMININE* MEANS TO ME:** Sisterhood savant.

Service
**Work. Philanthropy.**
+
Wealth
**Income. Outflow.**

*Counts pennies. Counts blessings.*
*Money in the cookie jar.*
*Stock portfolio.*
*Broke.*
*Gives at the office. Gives at church.*
*More than enough. Just enough.*
*Lives lightly on the land.*
*Owns. Lends. Offers.*
*Creates the future one day at a time.*
*Wisdom of the elders.*
*Triple bottom line.*
*Emotionally bankrupt.*
*Trade secrets.*
*Thinks global. Buys local.*
*Ask and it is given.*
*Gives credit where credit is due.*
*Can't take it with you when you leave.*
*Have your cake and eat it too.*
*Plenty.*

# What Works Well for Me

IF I WAS GUARANTEED TO BE VOCATIONALLY SUCCESSFUL AND ALL OF MY FINANCIAL NEEDS WOULD BE MET,
I WOULD: (OR IF I WERE TO START MY CAREER ALL OVER AGAIN, I WOULD:)

MY OWN FORM OF SPECIAL GENIUS IS:

THE TOOLS OF MY TRADE ARE:

THE PEOPLE I INTERACT WITH THE MOST FOR WORK PROBABLY SEE ME AS SOMEONE WHO IS:

**MY MONEY ROLE MODELS ARE:**

**BECAUSE THEY:**

**IF I WERE GOING TO WRITE A BRILLIANT BOOK IT WOULD BE ABOUT:**

*What do you have to say, to pass on, or to talk about with passion?*

**OUT OF ALL THE CHARITIES AND CAUSES IN THE WORLD, WHAT PULLS AT MY HEARTSTRINGS MOST IS:**

**MY PURPOSE IN LIFE IS:**

*If you're searching for your purpose, try this: "I would love it if God called me up and told me that my purpose in life is":*

**I AM VERY INTERESTED, FASCINATED, AND INTRIGUED BY:**

**BECAUSE:**

# Filter & Interpret your answers

What words or concepts feel important or intriguing to you?

What themes are showing up in your answers?

What words, images, or feelings are crossing your mind?

# What Does *Not* Work Well for Me

I FEEL UNCOMFORTABLE ABOUT MONEY WHEN:

MY IDEA OF A NIGHTMARE JOB IS:

BECAUSE IT WOULD MAKE ME FEEL:

I TEND TO GET STINGY ABOUT:

MY WORST FINANCIAL CHOICE:

BECAUSE:

# Filter & Interpret your answers

What words or concepts **feel important or intriguing** to you?

What **themes** are showing up in your answers?

What **words, images, or feelings** are crossing your mind?

ENDURING
BOLD

DESIGNED
EASE

## Kate Stevenson, March 1968
### *Mother. Writer.*

## Andrew Williamson, January 1972
### *Father. Filmmaker.*

### *Enduring*

**SPIRIT:** Tough cookies, rugged, unwavering, devoted, and ultimately pragmatic, Enduring is profoundly patient and can stay the course with a steady heart and mind. Whether socially conventional or rebellious, Enduring has a great sense of dignity, pride, and principles. When Enduring commits, they do so wholeheartedly and with certainty. Never one to back down from adversity or conflict, Enduring stands up to support friends, mates, and chosen causes. Leaders and stewards of ideas, Enduring can be equally effective and at ease in a team or independently. The shadow side of Enduring is unyielding stubbornness and a tendency to suffer or tolerate "too much" without taking positive action. Enduring generously gives and openly receives acknowledgment and recognition.

**LOOK & FEEL:** The spectrum of Enduring ranges from timeless pieces drawn from ancient cultures and classic tradition to street-smart and rugged. Solid, durable, tightly woven, heavy-duty textiles; chunky, sturdy, dark, bold, storytelling.

### *Bold*

*adventurous, assuming, audacious, brash, brassy, brave, cheeky, clear, collected, confident, courageous, daring, dauntless, definite, dramatic, enterprising, evident, eye-catching, fearless, flashy, forceful, forward, fresh, gallant, heroic, imaginative, immodest, loud, nervy, plain, prominent, pronounced, resolute, self-possessed, sassy, shameless, showy, smart, spirited, strong, valiant, vivid*

### *Designed*

**SPIRIT:** Designed absolutely, positively adores simplicity and things that "make the most sense." They applaud original thinking and effective systems and are innately innovative, inventive, strategic, and intentional. Designed loves to know what the plan is or to improve on it. In pursuit of solutions or creativity, Designed can be an excellent researcher, networker, brainstormer, and visionary. They seek out contemporaries and modernizers to nourish their spirit and intellect. On a bad day, Designed can be overly willful or get stuck on the details of a strategy. They strive for mastery and excellence in focused areas. Visual expression is frequently of utmost importance to Designed. They are sincerely open to new ideas and ways of doing things, yet confident in their own perspectives and opinions. Designed dispenses advice when asked but does so with tremendous consideration and restraint.

**LOOK & FEEL:** Modern, contemporary; could be futuristic. Tailored, custom-made, architectural. Designed loves patterns, graphics, icons, simplified complexity, and symbols. Appreciate state-of-the-art, handcrafted, and efficient construction.

### *Ease*

*affluence, calm, comfort, contentment, enjoyment, flow, genuine, grace, happiness, leisure, luxury, natural, organic, prosperity, quietness, quietude, relaxation, repose, rest, satisfaction, security, serenity, sway, tranquility*

## KATE

**I AM ATTRACTED TO:** Morocco—the completely exotic clash of cultures.

**ONE OUTFIT FOR THE REST OF MY LIFE:** A long, flowing gown of some sort, like a stylized caftan, with a huge choker necklace.

**I FEEL AT HOME IN:** Paris, where the people are introverted but loyal.

**I FEEL STIFLED BY:** grayness.

**THE TOOLS OF MY TRADE ARE:** dreams, courage, a keyboard.

**MY IDEA OF A NIGHTMARE JOB:** Accounting assistant for IBM.

**BEAUTY IS:** truth.

**I CRAVE:** freedom.

**MY FRIENDS:** are women of all ages.

**I LOVE TO TALK ABOUT:** anything.

**I SECRETLY LOVE:** I don't love anything secretly.

**MY FAVORITE BAND:** Hybrid.

**MOVIES THAT INSPIRED ME:** *Wall Street* and *Muriel's Wedding.*

**I'M SCARED:** of the inability to imagine.

**WHEN I'M AN OLD LADY:** I will be simplified down—but bold and looking very well traveled.

**ENDURING MEANS TO ME:** Hanging in there, like a cockroach or a rock.

**BOLD MEANS TO ME:** Not afraid to make a statement while doing so.

## ANDREW

**OBJECTS I CHERISH:** My wedding ring. My Mac. The bus. Any smart design that makes life easier and simpler.

**ONE OUTFIT FOR THE REST OF MY LIFE:** A very simple modern suit—gray or brown. I'm a uniform dresser.

**I LISTEN TO:** KCRW.org; music with strong lyrics. Beck, Tori Amos, Johnny Cash—it's got to be meaningful.

**MY OWN FORM OF GENIUS:** is diplomacy.

**MY EXERCISE IS:** yoga, walking.

**I DO WHAT I DO:** because film is a medium that entertains while affecting change.

**I FEEL MOST AT HOME:** walking by the ocean. The "outside" matches my "inside," allowing for peace and contemplation.

**MY FAVORITE TV SHOWS ARE:** *Twin Peaks* and *Buffy the Vampire Slayer*—strange, engaging, compelling, and mysterious.

**MY PHILOSOPHY ON FRIENDSHIP IS:** that friends make a life.

**DESIGNED MEANS TO ME:** Putting work into making something right.

**EASE MEANS TO ME:** Reaping the rewards.

**CLOCKWISE:** Turkish apple teaspoons; name plates from our childhood bedrooms; Scotch—Andrew's favorite gift to receive; custom-made pillow, Turkish teacup, Middle Eastern coffeepot; camel bags converted into cushions—we bought them with some wedding money; Lilah Blue's dress; milk chocolate Pocky Sticks

Relationships
**Friends. Romance.**
**Family. Colleagues.**
**+**
Communication
**Tools for interacting.**

*Tools for interacting.*

*Soul mate. Playmate.*

*Born to lead.*

*Extrovert.*

*Arrested development.*

*Forgiveness.*

*Couples counseling.*

*Consistency.*

*Thank-you cards.*

*Cross-promotional marketing strategies.*

*Ego driven.*

*Analog vs. digital.*

*Clams up. Works the room.*

*Grand, sweeping gestures.*

*A short note that says it all.*

*Receptive.*

*Unapologetic.*

*Every word is true.*

# What Works Well for Me

MY PHILOSOPHY ON FRIENDSHIP IS:

I AM THE KIND OF FRIEND WHO:

MY LIKE-MINDED FRIENDS, COMMUNITY, AND TRIBE ARE:

THEY ARE THE TYPE OF PEOPLE WHO:

# What Does *Not* Work Well for Me

I FEEL STIFLED BY/WHEN:

MY GREATEST HEARTBREAK WAS BECAUSE:

I AM MOST ANNOYED BY PEOPLE WHO:

I HAVE VERY LITTLE TOLERANCE FOR:

I WITHHOLD MY LOVE WHEN:

WHICH MAKES ME FEEL:

# Filter & Interpret your answers

What words or concepts **feel important or intriguing** to you?

What **themes** are showing up in your answers?

What **words, images, or feelings** are crossing your mind?

NATURAL
COSMOPOLITAN

FEMININE
DRAMATIC

# DEFINITION

## Victoria Roberts, April 1960
### *Founder, Zovo Lingerie Company.*

## Dorothea Roberts, May 1930
### *Retired Educator/Counselor.*

### *Natural*

**SPIRIT:** Natural is genuine, free from artificiality, affectation, and inhibitions. Natural is known for being spontaneous and easygoing. Natural hates to be fenced in and riles against conformity and unreasonable rules, though they are rooted in moral certainty and a strong sense of justice. Very much at ease with their essential selves, Natural is often very instinctive, sensuous, or highly sexual. They aren't strangers to hedonism or pleasure seeking. They love to get down to basics and can be graceful and direct communicators. Down to earth, literally and figuratively, Natural has a deep reverence and respect for nature and ecological systems, which delights and replenishes them, and an appreciation of supernatural forces.

**LOOK & FEEL:** All things generated by nature: wood, minerals, gems. Natural coloring, textiles, and produce. Rustic, primitive, flowing, native, or common to its surroundings.

### *Cosmopolitan*

*advanced, connected, contemporary, cultivated, cultured, current, flexible, freethinking, global, gregarious, indulgent, in fashion, latest, liberal, linked, metropolitan, modern, new, open-minded, permissive, polished, present, progressive, responsive, smooth, sophisticated, synchronous, tolerant, topical, worldly*

### *Feminine*

**SPIRIT:** Feminine is a force to be reckoned with—sheer womanpower. They are nurturing, inclusive, and intrinsically and actively compassionate. Midwives and caretakers of ideas and community, Feminine is often sought out for guidance, inspiration, and comfort. In full bloom, she has a great sense of adventure, as well as a healthy balance of responsibility. Feminine regularly exercises her prerogative to change her mind, start over, or wait it out. Sometimes Feminine can struggle with excessive or repressed emotion, thereby denying herself and those around her the full richness of her significant power. Feminine's holistic, often metaphysical perspective on life honors spirituality as the key to fulfillment. By far, Feminine's greatest gift is her intuition. Her ability to sense the truth of what's happening or what is to come is an incredibly effective tool for creating desirable realities.

**LOOK & FEEL:** All things woman: shapeliness, curves, softness. Sumptuous, luxurious, generous, comfortable, fluid. Tends to be ornate or artistic. Florals, flourish, color. Light, sparkling, radiance.

### *Dramatic*

*affecting, breathtaking, change agent, climactic, cultivated, effective, elegant, exciting, expressive, forceful, glamorous, harmonious, impactful, influential, inspired, meaningful, passionate, performer, persuasive, poetic, powerful, results, sensitive, striking, sublime, tasteful, thespian, thrilling, vivid, visible, voice*

## VICTORIA

**I LOVE:** my store and all things Zovo; my wedding ring; nag champa incense, five-star hotels, Marni dresses, yoga, my BlackBerry, dancing in my living room, candles, my dog, Survivor, strong coffee, and to belly laugh.

**ART THAT HAS INSPIRED ME:** Michelangelo's *David*, bullfighting, fly-fishing, golf, Dylan, Hemingway, the Beatles, Zeppelin, and Hank Williams.

**MY FAVORITE PIECE OF CLOTHING:** My Zovo cotton panties and my old leather motorcycle jacket.

**TWENTY-FOUR OF BLISS:** Taking my husband salmon fishing in the morning, shopping in Florence in the afternoon, and ending the day in the first-class section of the Orient Express heading to St. Petersburg in the middle of winter, enjoying a huge meal with the finest wines.

**MY DREAM CAREER:** I'd have Keith Richards's career.

**MY DEFINITION OF SEXY IS:** matadors and cowboys.

**MY MOTHER WOULD SAY:** I asked her. She said, "You are indomitable, invincible, compassionate, and ingenious." What can I say? She's Feminine Dramatic.

***NATURAL* MEANS TO ME:** Being open, free-spirited, and connected with nature. It's the feeling of cotton.

***COSMOPOLITAN* MEANS TO ME:** Connecting with people, different experiences, places, learning new things about the world, and feeling beautiful. It's the feeling of silk.

## DOROTHEA

**I LOVE:** the gift of life and I treasure it, each and every moment! My husband of fifty-five years, my four daughters, my sons-in-law, and my six perfect grandchildren. I love peace, beauty, and tranquility. I love the sunsets, the snowcapped mountains, the movement of water, the eagle that visits me every day for his "fix" (a turkey leg that I feed him). I love the space I made for relaxing and meditating; the Blessed Mother, of course, is a highlight.

**MY "INNER" AGE IS REALLY:** midthirties! Attitude, attitude!

**MY DREAM CAREER:** At one time, when "really young," was to sing like Doris Day and be a headliner with one of the popular dance bands. However, now my dream career would be as a talk show headliner, as that would be the greatest way to reach so many young women. Educating women to the fact that they do not have to take the abuse that happens to them is of utmost importance!

**I HAVE VERY LITTLE TOLERANCE FOR:** stupidity. I do not mind ignorance, but being a fool is not necessary in this day and age.

**MY PURPOSE IN LIFE:** is to be a good role model for my children, grandchildren, and others that I know. I believe that what we sow, we shall reap (for sure!).

***FEMININE* MEANS TO ME:** Equality with masculine.

***DRAMATIC* MEANS TO ME:** Vocalizing my travels and adventures and the many incidents with gusto

**VICTORIA:** Panerai watch, Floret perfume, black halter dress, hiking boot, golf ball (the purest sport I know), hunting hat (the ultimate nature experience is waking up with the animals at first light). **DOROTHEA:** Mother Mary statuette—beautiful, serene, and there to talk to; Hawaii figurine (so many times I have seen women on guys' dashboards and it was so sexist to me that I had my fun by getting a guy hula dancer for my dashboard; Aldolfo jacket I bought over fifty years ago, coin earrings, meditation pillow.

Creativity
Ideas. Creations.
+
Celebration
Occasions. Gifts.

*A blank canvas.*

*Happy birthday to you.*

*Techno-bass boom beats.*

*Journals. Pasted-in ticket stubs. Paint chips.*

*Backyard barbecue.*

*With this ring...*

*One thousand customers served.*

*Brings tears to your eyes.*

*Originality. Liberation. Controversy.*

*Mixed media.*

*Buckets of gladiolas.*

*Handmade invitations.*

*Just the two of you on a hill.*

*The Golden mean.*

*Stark. Abstract. Alchemical.*

*Pure logic rearranged.*

*From nothing comes something.*

*Simply lyrical.*

*First kiss.*

*Life is short.*

*The more, the merrier.*

# What Works Well for Me

**THE ULTIMATE CELEBRATION OR PARTY THAT I'D LIKE TO THROW WOULD BE:**

*It can be for something that hasn't yet occurred but you'd like to have happen—any reason you want.*

**I EXPRESS MY MENTAL CREATIVITY IN THE WAY I:**

**I EXPRESS MY PHYSICAL CREATIVITY IN THE WAY I:**

**MY MUSE AND INSPIRATION ARE:**

**WHEN I AM INSPIRED MY MIND FEELS:**

WHEN I AM INSPIRED MY BODY FEELS:

THE BEST MATERIAL GIFT I'VE EVER RECEIVED:
I CHERISH IT BECAUSE:

MY FAVORITE MUSICIANS, SINGERS, OR BANDS ARE:
BECAUSE THEY ARE:
AND THEIR MUSIC IS:

THE PERFORMER THAT I'D SECRETLY LOVE TO BE LIKE, OR CAN RELATE TO IS:
BECAUSE:

SOME ARTISTS (ACTORS, PAINTERS, FILMMAKERS, ARCHITECTS) AND/OR WORKS OF ART THAT HAVE MOVED
ME DEEPLY ARE:
BECAUSE I WAS SO IMPRESSED BY:

# Filter & Interpret your answers

What words or concepts feel important or intriguing to you?

What themes are showing up in your answers?

What words, images, or feelings are crossing your mind?

# What Does *Not* Work Well for Me

SOME OF THE BANDS OR ACTORS WHO DO NOTHING FOR ME OR MAKE ME CRINGE ARE:

BECAUSE:

THE MOST INAPPROPRIATE GIFT SOMEONE COULD GIVE ME WOULD BE:

BECAUSE:

MY INNER CRITIC MAKES ME SHRINK BY TELLING ME:

I STOP MYSELF FROM BEING EXPRESSIVE WHEN:

AND THE RESULT IS:

# Filter & Interpret your answers

What words or concepts **feel important or intriguing** to you?

What **themes** are showing up in your answers?

What **words, images, or feelings** are crossing your mind?

GENTEEL
VITALITY

## Joan Pham, October 1983

*Nurse.*

### Genteel

**SPIRIT:** Genteel is the ultimate lady. Quietly powerful, she is poised, dignified, and well mannered. She may speak softly, but Genteel's words are chosen very mindfully and purposefully—her ethics and morals are as strong as her loving heart. Genteel feels a great sense of devotion to her family and heritage. She is a natural healer. She loves to foster ideas and to develop and implement the most elegant and sensible way of doing things. She prefers to know as much as she possibly can about what interests her. Genteel is an excellent hostess and loves to give and receive gifts. When she is out of sync with her own inner voice, Genteel may become overly accommodating and silent or confined by her own rules. But it is the combination of sensitivity and dignified poise that makes for her resolute character. Genteel's forms of feminine power can range from honoring traditions to enterprising, women-based solutions to freedom of sexual expression.

**LOOK & FEEL:** Undeniably feminine, sophisticated, sensual, calm, gentle. Sacred objects, tranquil sanctuaries, and places of devotion. Proper manners and traditional celebrations. Often appreciates flowing, graceful materials. Loves lingerie.

### Vitality

*bloom, bold, bounce, continuity, color, creativity, drive, energetic, energy, exuberance, fervor, force, generosity, guts, inspiration, intensity, life, life-affirming, life force, liveliness, moxy, power, pulse, sparkle, spirit, spunk, strength, verve, vigor, vim, virility, vivaciousness*

**CLOCKWISE:** Mechanical pencil (a gift from Rachel), my journal—the entranceway to my quiet time and a cache for dreams; belly dancing hip chain, cat figurine, wood comb given to me by my father when he went back to Vietnam for the first time, chocolate milk, pasties (the height of joy in a burlesque act is when the pasties are a-twirlin'!), calligraphy ink

**I LOVE:** how each person is a universe.

**I WANT TO TRAVEL TO:** Vietnam to seek out my roots and to travel in the beauty of the lotus fields.

**I WOULD LIKE TO MASTER:** the art of healing. Not in a quick-fix way but, rather, helping people to become skilled and insightful at healing and empowering themselves.

**ARTWORK I'D BRING INTO MY DREAM HOME:** A Quan Yin statue. Pieces that would generate serenity.

**I AM REPELLED BY:** the intention to inflict pain. Malice. Things that are too busy—visual dissonance.

**I LIKE THE FASHION OF:** Reese Witherspoon. Peep-toe shoes. Fine tailored, waist-cinching jackets with a feminine touch. Audrey Hepburn: classic feminine elegance. Gwen Stefani: creative, daring, innovative, and still feminine.

**I LONG TO:** use my voice more, to say what I think, and to trust that my words are sincere and heartfelt, rather than scrutinizing to death what I'd like to say for fear I'll hurt or offend the other person. I'm done with that.

**I EXPRESS MY CREATIVITY:** burlesque dancing, journaling.

**MY BELIEF SYSTEM IS:** roughly stated, Love.

**I WANT:** to keep becoming, resonating authenticity. To get my next belt in kickboxing. Eventually to become a vegan. To create. To completely and totally open myself up to the world, to love and continue to bloom and see where my niche is in life. To soak in the textures, the feelings of everyday life (and find the light, the sparkle that underlies us all).

**FAVORITE SCENT:** Jasmine. Rose water. Clean air.

**FAVORITE MOVIES:** *Little Women* and *Amélie*.

**YOU COULDN'T PAY ME ENOUGH TO:** spend a lot of time on something that I don't believe in.

***GENTEEL* MEANS TO ME:** Consideration of others in a classic chivalrous manner. Refinement; a wee bit of reservation, if only initially. To be gracious; honor.

***VITALITY* MEANS TO ME:** Having a big old grand time; laughing. Green. Sparkle, gusto, courage, empowered zest. Cheeky and saucy. Awareness, life force, throbbing rhythm to continue forward, upward, and creatively. It's the sparkle in the eyes.

Body
Food. Exercise.

+

Wellness
Care and healing.

*Care and healing.*
*Proud.*
*Tribal tattoos.*
*Comfortable in her own skin.*
*Sun worshipper.*
*Never leaves home without lipstick.*
*Closely shaved.*
*Implants. Reduction.*
*Birthed two babies.*
*Bodacious and loving it.*
*Tweezed.*
*Face like a road map.*
*Built to last.*
*Antioxidants. Anti-aging.*
*Eco-friendly.*
*Green with envy.*
*Wild child.*
*On the surface. Deep tissue.*
*Radiant.*
*Like a temple.*

# What Works Well for Me

WHEN I HAVE FREE TIME I FEEL:

I DESCRIBE MY INNER RHYTHM AS:

A FEW THINGS THAT I APPRECIATE ABOUT MY BODY:

IF I COULD GET A TATTOO THAT COULD BE REMOVED AT ANYTIME, I WOULD GET:

BECAUSE IT:

MY IDEAL BODY FEELS:




MY PREFERRED FORM OF EXERCISE IS:




IT WORKS FOR ME BECAUSE:




IF I COULD WIN AN OLYMPIC MEDAL, I WOULD WANT IT TO BE FOR:




BECAUSE THAT SPORT IS ABSOLUTELY:

# Filter & Interpret your answers

What words or concepts **feel important or intriguing** to you?

What **themes** are showing up in your answers?

What **words, images, or feelings** are crossing your mind?

# What Does *Not* Work Well for Me

WHEN I AM OVERTAXED MY BODY FEELS:

I TRY TO HIDE MY:

BECAUSE I FEEL:

IF I RESIST EXERCISE IT'S BECAUSE:

WHEN I OVERDO IT PHYSICALLY, IT'S USUALLY IN THE FORM OF:

WHEN I NEGLECT MY WELL-BEING, I END UP FEELING:

# Filter & Interpret your answers

What words or concepts **feel important or intriguing** to you?

What **themes** are showing up in your answers?

What **words, images, or feelings** are crossing your mind?

CLASSIC
HARMONY

# Lyn Connock, March 1946

*Education Editor. Researcher.*

## Classic

**SPIRIT:** Classic chooses quality, lasting and enduring value, and experiences, people, and things from the highest rank or class. Classic is known and appreciated for being cordial, refined, and somewhat formal. They feel somewhat romantic about the past and often appreciate and respect tradition. Because they strive for excellence and perfection, they do their homework and practice due diligence. They are great at getting the most out of a system and will typically seek out authoritative advice and choose established or recognized standards rather than experimental or futuristic options. Their decisions are measured and certain. They have a sense of nobility, err on the side of convention, and take pride in their principles and values. The shadow side of Classic can be overly controlled or restrained. Classic loves to nurture and support things that will have lasting significance and value or the potential to create a legacy.

**LOOK & FEEL:** Classic goes for the best. Quality, top of its class, superior. Simplified and harmonious. Restrained, conservative, elegant. Having historical or legendary associations.

## Harmony

*accord, affinity, agreement, amicability, combination, compatibility, concord, conformity, consensus, consistency, cooperation, correspondence, ease, empathy, flow, friendship, grace, goodwill, home, kinship, like-mindedness, peace, progressives, rapport, sympathy, tranquility, understanding, unity*

**CLOCKWISE:** Commissioned silk-screen portrait of our cat Lionel, Hamley Bear, L'eau d'Issey, World Wildlife Fund bag, the poetry of Emily Dickinson, *Persuasion* by Jane Austen, *The Colony of Unrequited Dreams* by Wayne Johnston, *The Botany of Desire* by Michael Pollan, passport, Dartington crystal holder and full-blown rose, hand-woven pillow, betrothal ring

**I LOVE:** the life that my husband and I have created, which includes wonderful family and friends. Animals and the environment. The theater, from Shakespeare to contemporary plays. Visiting new and revisiting favorite places.

**MY DREAM HOME:** I'm content with many things and am seeking different things at this stage of my life, so a dream house is not at the top of my list.

**ART THAT INSPIRES ME:** An absolutely beautifully played piece of music can bring me to tears.

**PHILOSOPHY ON FRIENDSHIP:** It's precious. Ideally, it is freely given, able to withstand a little abuse. It should be sustaining for both in the friendship—for the one who is currently giving and for the one who will be giving next week.

**I FEEL TERRIFIC WEARING:** an evening skirt and jacket I had made from silk I bought in Thailand.

**BOOKS THAT HELPED DEFINE MY LIFE:** the novels of Jane Austen and the poetry of Emily Dickinson have helped me through dark times.

**A RITE OF PASSAGE IN MY LIFE WAS:** surviving cancer. It made me aware of what is really important—a cliché but true.

**I WOULD LIKE TO REVOLUTIONIZE:** environmental awareness.

**I AM UNINTERESTED IN:** the cult of celebrity.

**IN MY DEEPEST BEING:** I wonder about paths not taken.

***CLASSIC* MEANS TO ME:** Proportion, impact, longevity. Things that have a history and have stood the test of time—we know that they're lovely and worthy of respect and caring.

***HARMONY* MEANS TO ME:** The pleasing effect of balance. When things are in harmony, you can soar.

## Nature
The elements.
+
## Rest & Relaxation
What calms and entertains you.

*Rocky Mountain high.*

*Palm trees.*

*Summer thunderstorms.*

*Pink Floyd on the headphones in the dark.*

*Hot bath. Hot chocolate. Hot rocks.*

*Turn off the ringer. Call your best friend.*

*Vipassana. Sermons. Walt Whitman.*

*Mother Earth. Gaia. Natura.*

*In silence I hear my soul.*

*Reduce. Reuse. Recycle.*

*Cycle to work.*

*Herbal tea. Stiff scotch.*

*Humane shelter mutts. Eagles. Elephants.*

*Watercolor class.*

*Going fast.*

*Falling leaves.*

*Taking stock.*

*When the tide is high.*

# What Works Well for Me

**MY FAVORITE FLOWER IS:**

**IF THIS FLOWER HAD ITS OWN PERSONALITY, I WOULD DESCRIBE IT AS:**

**MY FAVORITE TIME OF YEAR IS:**

*What do you love about it? What feelings does that season evoke in you?*

**I EXPRESS MY REVERENCE FOR NATURE, ANIMALS, AND ECOLOGY BY:**

WHAT I TREASURE MOST ABOUT THE EARTH WE LIVE ON IS:

MY FAVORITE PASTIME OR HOBBY IS:
BECAUSE:

MY FAVORITE TV SHOWS ARE:

I DIG THEM BECAUSE:

MY FAVORITE FORM OF PLAY IS:

# Filter & Interpret your answers

What words or concepts **feel important or intriguing** to you?

What **themes** are showing up in your answers?

What **words, images, or feelings** are crossing your mind?

# What Does *Not* Work Well for Me

**WHEN I DON'T GET ENOUGH R & R, I:**

**TOO MUCH:**

**MAKES ME:**

**I AM COMPLETELY UNINTERESTED IN OR BORED BY:**

**I GET REALLY UPTIGHT OR UNCOMFORTABLE:**

# Filter & Interpret your answers

What words or concepts **feel important or intriguing** to you?

What **themes** are showing up in your answers?

What **words, images, or feelings** are crossing your mind?

I am looking for the face I had before the world was made.

—WILLIAM BUTLER YEATS

# Define

## Part 3

# DEFINING YOUR STYLE STATEMENT

# This is the moment we've all been waiting for.

Honor how important your Style Statement could be for you. Claim your truth. Weave some words into the focal point of your greatness.

# Helpful Hints

**USE THE RESOURCES.** The Style Vocabulary that begins on page 233 mostly represents Foundation Word possibilities—the first word of your Style Statement, your being, your 80%. Each definition is a story unto itself—a small personality poem that captures some of the layers of your essence. These are the words that have shown up most frequently in other people's Style Statements—based on our experience with hundreds of clients and readers. As archetypes, they reflect significant themes and aesthetic tastes for many people. And they can be used to describe the spirit, look, and feel of someone or something. The Style Vocabulary is a key tool in choosing useful Style Statement words.

The Style Vocabulary is not exhaustive. We encourage you to look for the best-fitting words for your true self, even if those words do not appear in our list.

A standard dictionary or thesaurus could come in very handy at this stage. We also recommend dictionary.com, which offers a thesaurus and provides the origins and history of many words.

**BE PRECISE.** To state the obvious, the definition of each of your Style Statement words is of monumental importance. Subtleties, nuances, and double entendres can make for very powerful formulas. Also, if your first or favorite language is not English, and if it feels more meaningful to do so, you can certainly create your Style Statement in another language.

Very mindfully, study the definitions of the words that resonate with you. Every word represents a universe of possibility.

**LOOK FOR CONTRAST.** Your two words may be in extreme contrast with each other, perhaps even paradoxical. Such a combination could be ideal. For example, Modern Heritage, Tailored Freedom, Composed Dramatic. Together, these concepts may seem like polar opposites, but it is just this kind of creative tension and contrast that makes for integrated, wholehearted living.

**SPEAK YOUR SPIRIT.** Your Style Statement is where spirit meets matter, where your heart meets your head, and

your image and persona meet the real you. The deeper meaning is as important as the surface details.

**MAKE IT PERSONAL.** Your Style Statement only has to work for you. This is the name you give yourself, and only you—not your friends, your mother, or a salesclerk—need to know why it fits so perfectly.

**IT'S A FRESH START.** Though your Style Statement is a reflection of your true essence, if you've been living out of sync with yourself, it may not bear much resemblance to your past. Your Style Statement is a clarion call for the life that you want to create now and are moving toward.

**IT'S ALWAYS TRUE.** Perhaps your Style Statement beautifully sums up the wisest choices you've made along the way, or it represents who you've always been but were never able to put into words.

**FOLLOW YOUR ASPIRATION.** A Style Statement is designed to move you forward. Maybe your Style Statement isn't who you are 24/7, but it is most definitely who you are when you are being your whole self. Think highly of yourself, and the world will respond accordingly.

# The 80/20 Style Statement Principle:
## A Refresher

Accomplish more with less.

Focusing on the right things creates the biggest results.

Volumes have been written on the 80/20 principle. Some theorists believe that this ratio fundamentally explains how the universe works. Developed by Italian economist Vilfredo Pareto, the Pareto principle, which states that 80% of the outcome is created from just 20% of the input, is a heartily embraced concept in business management. For example, 80% of the total revenue is often generated from 20% of the clientele or product line. So it makes the most sense to focus your efforts on the 20% of the people (or products, services, activities, or time) that create the biggest impact.

## YOUR 80% FOUNDATION

This is the core of who you are, your essential self. This is the part of you that feels like first nature, even if you resist it. It is the part of you that is often the most obvious and steady. It shows up in what you most strongly believe, in what you most often choose, and in the most frequent themes of your fashion and taste in decor. For many people, it's easy to express and practice the spirit of their foundation word. For others, it represents an aspect of their life that they need to give themselves full permission to embrace and to be. (See Foundation Words on page 233.)

## YOUR 20% CREATIVE EDGE

Your creative edge makes all the difference and is what moves you forward. In keeping with the 80/20 principle, it's your 20% that goes out and gets the results. It also tends to be a trigger for our greatest lessons and struggles. For example, we may be longing for all the great stuff that Harmony or Play or Adventure brings

us. And yet it may be that our personal blocks are wrapped up in being harmonious or playful or adventurous. We tend to either repress or overcompensate with our creative edge.

Your foundation word represents your being. Your creative edge is how you express and distinguish your being. In terms of aesthetics, it's your accessories and your accent pieces. It's your jewelry or the artwork on your walls. It's a touch of color in your hair or the red leather boots that say, I can be wild when I wanna be.

In terms of your spirit and the way you relate, your creative edge is most often the impression that you make. It's what drives and inspires you. And the beauty of the 80/20 principle in this case is that you don't have to be living on your creative edge at all times. In fact, to do so would lead to overkill and burnout. Think of your creative edge as a powerful force—a little bit goes a long way.

# It's All About You:
## Defining Your Style Statement

### Step 1: Take Out the Garbage

Review the "What does not work for me" section from each lifestyle domain inquiry. **Collect the outstanding words and themes from those sections, and write them in the space below.** Add anything new that occurs to you. If you are fundamentally bugged by something, can't stand it, loathe it—now is your chance to let it rip.

These words and thoughts will likely convey a meaning that is opposite of your Style Statement. They are in conflict with who you truly are or aspire to be.

# Step 2: Take a Breather

Breathe in. Breathe out. One more time, from your belly. And, again. Now, read these words with feeling. From the depth of your heart:

*My Style Statement names my essence.*
*It resonates with the true me, the whole me, me at my best.*
*My Style Statement claims my greatest potential.*
*My Style Statement communicates how amazing I am.*

This is not the time to be modest, act small, or fear grandiosity. This is your party. Rise to the occasion. Imagine what is possible. Surpass your expectations. Think highly of yourself!

Free your mind, and the rest will follow. Your Style Statement will move you forward.

- If you feel yourself shying away from words that seem "too big" or "too special," then it's time to expand your perspective.
- If some words ring true but aren't who you've been or how other people may see you, then take one step forward and away from your past.
- Or if a word feels clear and sincere to you but sounds just too basic or too ordinary, remember the power of simplicity.

Now, steady as you go.

# Step 3: Count Your Blessings

Review the "What works well for me" section from each lifestyle domain inquiry. **Collect the outstanding words and themes from those sections, and write them in the space below.** Add anything new that occurs to you. Listen to your inner voice. Include everything. Write any new words or ideas that flow into your mind. Don't censor yourself. Don't tiptoe around your insights. Be brave and be free.

These words and thoughts are the stepping-stones to your Style Statement. Your Style Statement may be a combination of these exact words, or it may be a pair of similar words that hasn't yet occurred to you. Keep going. You're getting closer.

# Step 4: Make Some Choices and Connections

THE PURPOSE OF A STYLE STATEMENT, AS YOU KNOW BY NOW, IS TO HELP YOUR EXTERIOR REFLECT YOUR INTERIOR. THEREFORE, ONE WORD HAS TO APPLY TO BOTH THE MATERIAL AND THE IMMATERIAL BECAUSE YOU CAN'T HAVE, SAY, A "CONFIDENT" SOFA OR AN "ECLECTIC" HAIRSTYLE.

**From the collection of words in Step 3, choose three to five words that have the strongest resonance and attraction for you, and write them in the grid below.** At least two of these words must be applicable to material things.

Refer to the Style Vocabulary at the back of the book or consult a dictionary for inspiration and clarity.

| THE WORD | SYNONYMS |
|----------|----------|
| 1. | 1. |
| 2. | 2. |
| 3. | 3. |
| 4. | 4. |
| 5. | 5. |

**Record the synonyms associated with each word you listed.** This is a very important step. Seeing related words expands your perspective. Refer to the Style Vocabulary at the back of the book, or consult a thesaurus. Look behind the words. Pay attention to what moves you.

# Step 5: Look Closer: Tune in to Your Feelings

Have you discovered any synonyms that feel like they might be part of your Style Statement? The new words that surface at this stage might be part of your magic combination. Newly found synonyms often express what we sense about ourselves but have not yet clearly articulated. If it feels right, go with it. Remember: Be open. Be willing to surprise yourself with what's true.

**Now choose three or four words that feel like potential matches for you.**
Rewrite below any words that you've already listed, then add any new, additional words that surfaced in your synonym search. At least one of these words must be applicable to material things.

1.

2.

3.

4.

This latest collection of words should communicate the opposite of what showed up in your "What does not work for me" collection.

# Step 6: Focus and Shuffle

**Rewrite the three or four possible words from Step 5 in each column below, so the lists are identical.**

From the left column, cross out any word that cannot be used to describe a material object.

Also from the left column, cross out any word that seems like it would be too excessive, too far out, too uncomfortable, or too dramatic if it were 80% of your lifestyle.

From the right column, cross out any words that are still listed in the left column.

| POSSIBILITIES FOR YOUR **FOUNDATION** WORD (YOUR 80%) | POSSIBILITIES FOR YOUR **CREATIVE EDGE** WORD (YOUR 20%) |
|---|---|
| 1. | 1. |
| 2. | 2. |
| 3. | 3. |
| 4. | 4. |

# Step 7: Play with the Fit

**In the spaces below, rewrite the words left after Step 6.** These are your most likely Style Statement options.

If there are more than two words left, play with the combinations. Which combination feels right? Look back at the definition of each word.

**IF YOU'RE STUCK:**

- TAKE A BREAK. SOME DISCOVERIES HAPPEN IN PHASES, NOT ONE FELL SWOOP.
- CALL OR E-MAIL A FRIEND FOR SOME PERSPECTIVE.
- JOURNAL ABOUT YOUR "STUCKNESS"— FACING IT HEAD-ON OFTEN DISSOLVES THE BLOCK.
- SLEEP ON IT.
- LEAVE IT FOR A FEW DAYS, AND COME BACK TO IT FRESH.

**YOU'LL KNOW YOUR STYLE STATEMENT IS RIGHT WHEN:**

- YOU FEEL ENERGIZED RATHER THAN WEIGHED DOWN.
- YOU FEEL EXCITED.
- YOU FEEL WEEPY OR EMOTIONAL.
- YOU HAVE A SENSE OF CALM OR PEACE.
- YOU FEEL RELIEVED.
- YOU FEEL GRATITUDE AND APPRECIATION.
- YOU'RE SMILING.
- YOU FEEL SLIGHTLY UNCOMFORTABLE OR AWKWARD, BUT YOU FEEL IT'S RIGHT NONETHELESS.

......................................    ......................................

......................................    ......................................

......................................    ......................................

......................................    ......................................

Before you commit to your Style Statement, ask yourself if your Style Statement:

☐ Moves you forward. Does it feel like it's the truest possible description of you? Is it a name that you can live into and live up to? Is it you at your very best, your most natural, in your favorite state of being?

☐ Sounds like music to your ears. When it's right, it also sounds right. Do the words flow?

☐ Applies to both the spirit and the look and feel of something? Does it translate into a visual and material form? Here is the ultimate, and profoundly simple test of a Style Statement: Can it be used to describe your sofa and the way that you relate to people? Could it work for an outfit and your career?

☐ Makes you feel proud and elevated.

☐ Would make the people who know you best and love you the most say, "Of course! That's so you!"

# Step 8: Make It Official

**Rewrite the definitions and synonyms for each word to create your own Style Statement Profile.**

## *My Style Statement is:*

............................................................    ............................................................

        *(Foundation Word)*                  *(Creative Edge Word)*

As is your desire, so is your will.
As is your will, so is your deed.
As is your deed, so is your destiny.

—THE UPANISHADS

# Design

## Part 4

# DESIGNING YOUR LIFE: SEE IT,

You've discovered your Style Statement!

Now what?

Envision it.

Listen to it.

Let it seep into your bones.

# FEEL IT, BE IT

**Your Style Statement will be as useful as you make it.** It's a tool, and you're the craftsperson. You could use it to transform your entire life—to hone your talents into a lucrative livelihood, to declutter your mind and your living space, even to create more sincerity and intimacy in your relationships. Or you can use your Style Statement to figure out whether you should buy classic-fit Levi's or designer jeans. It's up to you.

## TIME-RELEASE CAPSULE

A few of us get our lessons in life-altering aha moments and lightning bolts. After discovering their Style Statements, some people make immediate overtures to toss out half their wardrobes, go blonde, look for a new job, and speak less and listen more. But for most of us, learning and change comes more gradually, in time-release capsules— new awareness, slowly building into a defining strength.

Revelations may pop up months after you've chosen your Style Statement. For example, *being too much Elegant and not enough Flow makes me too serious and less spontaneous. When I express my Vitality in staff meetings, we generate great ideas. Being more Tailored in my marriage means that I could actually create a plan to regularly connect with my partner.*

How many ways are there to express your Style Statement? Countless! Remember: You contain multitudes.

Every day is an opportunity to discover more of what it means to be you. And you can approach self-discovery like a writer methodically crafting a novel or like an Olympic athlete training to win the gold.

# Perspectives & Practice:
# 50 Ways to Express Your Style Statement

Following are a few perspectives and practice exercises to help bring your Style Statement—your whole self—to life. These are options, not orders. Play with them. Go at your own pace. Do only what gives you joy.

## HOME + STUFF

1. Edit. Let go of the things that don't match your Style Statement. Be ruthless. Purge! Liberate the true you. Go through your closet, your home, your to-do list, and your psyche, and get rid of anything that is cramping your style.

2. Make a date to visit furniture stores—both in and out of your price range—to explore what works with your Style Statement.

3. Create a special space with objects that represent and celebrate your essence.

4. Post your Style Statement on the refrigerator door or bathroom mirror.

5. Have your family crest or plaid researched.

6. Re-create. What can you revive in your home, wardrobe, or office that you have overlooked or neglected? Does your Style Statement inspire you to be a little more daring? Then frame that nude print in your attic, dig out your copy of *My Secret Garden,* rev up the old Mustang again. Everything we need is often right in front of us.

## FASHION + SENSUALITY

7. Scan fashion magazines for article titles containing one of your words.

8. Get together with other friends who have done their Style Statements, and have a Style Statement barter party, to trade items that it is time to let go of.

9. Get a tattoo that symbolizes your Style Statement. (Tattoo tip: think about it for at least six months, all the while looking high and low until you find a tattoo artist whose work you love.)

10. Let your hairdresser read your Style Statement definitions.

11. Go through all of your accessories, and let go of whatever is not truly your style.

12. Make an appointment to have a makeup consultation done. Many makeup stores and beauty counters offer this as a complimentary service.

13. Have something personalized with your Style Statement: stationery, jewelry, towels.

14. Create your own signature perfume with essential oils or by layering fragrances.

## SPIRIT + LEARNING

15. Create a style file. Begin to collect visuals of things that inspire you. Make a scrapbook, put together a collage, or store them in a shoe box. Magazines are fantastic sources of inspiration. Liberally tear out images of designs, colors, graphics, scenes, and looks that you are drawn to. Add fabric swatches, poems, postcards. And as you're collecting your ideals, know that the process helps to draw your fulfilled wishes to you.

16. Or start a really easy file-folder system. Label each file with the name of an area in the Lifestyle Map (e.g., Fashion, Home, Relationships), and file images and text that resonate with you in the appropriate folder. You can set up a similar virtual Style File on your computer to save documents, photographs, and links to Web sites.

17. Have something made for you. Commission a portrait. Bring your favorite magazine clippings of furniture or clothing to a carpenter or craftsperson.

18. Create a journal and use your Style Statement as an anchor in your daily reflections and future envisioning.

19. Do an Internet search for your Style Statement words, in combination and individually.

### SPIRIT + LEARNING

20. Go to the library and look up books that have one of your words in the title.

21. Take some personality assessments and see how they fit with your Style Statement. Try the Enneagram, the Meyers-Briggs, and the Strengths Finder Test.

22. Do a Style Statement retrospective of your life. Look at the highs and the lows of your past and see what aspects of your Style Statement were or were not in play at those times. Journaling about this can be very illuminating.

23. Write a Style Statement poem or a manifesto of your own Style Statement.

24. For twenty-one days in a row (because that's how long it takes to create a new habit), start or end your day by reading your Style Statement definitions.

### SERVICE + WEALTH

25. Hire an expert. Experts get paid for a reason. A few hundred bucks to an interior designer, a stylist, a personal organizer, a trainer, a coach, or a therapist could power quantum leaps in your life.

26. Write your Style Statement in your day timer at least once a week as a focal point for prioritizing.

27. Volunteer for a charitable cause that is in line with your heart.

28. Create a computer screensaver using your Style Statement words or definitions.

### RELATIONSHIPS + COMMUNICATION

29. Ask your partner to do his or her Style Statement, then unify your Style Statements to guide your relationship and home life. For example, Traditional Play and Simplistic Vitality could become Traditional Vitality or Simplistic Play. Find a combination of words that you are both happy with.

30. Start a Style Statement group or buddy system. Stay in touch with your friends who've done the Style Statement process and create ways to support each other in being all that you can be.

31. Create a logo that captures your Style Statement.

32. Register your Style Statement as a Web site domain name.

33. Don't tell anyone what your Style Statement is; keep it as your own secret weapon of self-expression.

34. Tell everyone what your Style Statement is. Call or e-mail your friends and let them know your latest discovery.

35. Create a new e-mail address using your Style Statement.

### CREATIVITY + CELEBRATION

36. Create an iPod music file to match the 80/20 balance of your Style Statement.

37. Do an Internet search combining one of your words with art—for example, Refined Art, Earth Art, Simplistic Art—and see what comes up.

38. Set an inspiration date for yourself. Visit an art gallery. Spend the afternoon in a news and magazine shop. Go window-shopping. Pay attention to what makes you feel up and what makes you feel down.

39. Do a Web search for quotes and songs with your words in them or for themes that you relate to.

40. Mark the date that you established your Style Statement in your calendar. On your one-year anniversary, review the past year and consider how your life has changed or improved.

### BODY + WELLNESS

41. Do an Internet search combining one of your words with Wellness—for example, Classic Wellness or Wellness Sophistication—and see what comes up.

42. Imagine. If your Style Statement were an Olympic event, what would it be?

43. Sign up for a dance lesson that suits your style—salsa, swing, ballroom, or ballet. You don't have to commit for weeks—it can be just one private class, but start somewhere.

44. Think about what type of fitness regimen aligns with your 20% word.

45. Even if you don't like to cook, peruse the cooking section of a bookstore and look for the ethnic dishes that appeal to you the most.

### NATURE + REST & RELAX

46. If your Style Statement were a major motion picture, what would the movie be about?

47. Go natural. What natural elements match your Style Statement? Beach tones, dark wood, or rare orchids on the kitchen windowsill? Go for a walk in the woods or down your streets. Look for objects that speak to you—a rock, a dented penny, a feather.

48. Meditate on your Style Statement. Feeling centered and still, ask your Style Statement to take form, and be open to any guidance, sensations, or images you might receive.

49. Visualize. Imagine that you open a door to a sacred room. The room is filled with all kinds of gifts that support your Style Statement, and they're all for you. What are they? How do you feel about receiving them? What will you do with them?

50. Imagine that your two words are traveling to you on rays of the sun. Fully absorb their warmth and intensity. Radiate their light as far as you can imagine.

# 5 Guiding Questions

When applied to any area of your life, these five questions could be revolutionary. This is a fabulous journaling exercise, one that you can do regularly.

Considering each area of the Lifestyle Map, ask yourself the following questions. If you were to do only this and no other Style Statement exercise, you would still make terrific progress in becoming more authentically you in every way.

1. **POSSIBILITY.** If anything were possible, what would you create in this area of your life?

2. **CHANGE.** What needs to be let go of in terms of your (insert lifestyle domain), both materially and emotionally?

3. **GRATITUDE.** What can be more appreciated in terms of your (insert lifestyle domain), both materially and emotionally?

4. **INSPIRATION.** Where and how do you find and give inspiration in this area of your life?

5. **AUTHENTICITY.** How can you more fully express your (insert lifestyle domain)?

# 3 Simple Things
# a Week

Every weekend, write down three simple things you will do to energize your Style Statement in the coming week.

1. **EDIT.** Let go of one thing—material objects, thoughts, or activities. It might be an old sweater, a pile of paper, a negative self-perception, or a small but nasty habit such as staying up too late or not recycling.

2. **ADD.** Bring in or reinvent one thing in your life—thoughts, activities, creations, objects.

3. **APPRECIATE.** More fully appreciate someone or something. Send a thank-you note to your partner, just for being your partner. Be extra polite to the guy who makes you latte. Get that old painting reframed and hung, or finally take those pants to the tailor. Spend some time admiring how beautiful your eyes are.

# Ask Yourself:
# A Journaling Exercise

Soak in your Style Statement words. Carefully examine each word and your definitions. Think about all of the seemingly abstract, nonfashion ways that your words can express themselves. Let your brain be loose and free to wander and wonder.

WHAT DOES MY STYLE STATEMENT AFFIRM ABOUT ME?

HOW DOES MY STYLE STATEMENT MAKE SENSE OF MY PAST?

WHEN OR WHERE IS IT EASIEST TO BE MY WHOLE SELF?

WHEN OR WHERE IS IT MOST DIFFICULT TO BE MY WHOLE SELF?

WHAT DO I RESIST ABOUT MY STYLE STATEMENT? WHERE IS MY LEARNING CURVE?

WHAT IN MY LIFE AND WHAT WAY OF BEING IS A CLEAR EXPRESSION OF MY STYLE STATEMENT?

WHAT IN MY LIFE IS OUT OF SYNC WITH MY STYLE STATEMENT?

IF I WERE BEING MY STYLE STATEMENT ALL OF THE TIME, IN EVERY WAY, IN A FEW YEARS, MY LIFE WOULD LOOK LIKE WHAT?

# A Few Reminders

**KNOW YOUR STRENGTHS.** What do you know the most about? What do you know the least about? Are you a culinary wizard but a hapless organizer? An art historian who can't navigate the Web? A sharp dresser who doesn't know the first thing about eyeliner? When you're clear about your expertise and your points of growth, you know when to ask for help and when to open yourself up to learning more.

**PRACTICE.** *At the top of a piece of paper, write these column headings and fill in your responses below them.*

**WHAT I'M GREAT AT:**

**WHAT I LOVE TO DO:**

**WHAT I STINK AT:**

**WHAT I LOATHE TO DO:**

What we're great at and what we love to do often go hand in hand. But, just because we excel at something doesn't mean we can't delegate it or get some support in that area. Ideally, we should spend our time and energy doing what we love to do, not what we think we have to do.

*On a separate page, write these three column headings, and categorize your previous answers into the areas where they fit best.*

**I WANT TO IMPROVE ON OR LEARN MORE ABOUT:**

**I NEED TO GET EXPERT SUPPORT OR DELEGATE:**

**IT WOULD HELP ME NOT TO WORRY ABOUT OR TO COMPLETELY LET GO OF:**

When you've looked at what you want to improve on, get support with, or let go of, make an easy plan to do just that. It could be as simple as some online research or as involved as a night class. As for getting expert support, don't let limitations such as time or money stand in your way. Getting help frees up time.

**SEEK INSPIRATION.** Expose yourself to art. People-watch. Create more contact with visual expression. Let yourself be moved. Sit down and color with your child, rent a foreign film instead of a Hollywood release, have lunch at an art college or at a gallery café.

**PRACTICE.** *Julia Cameron's timeless book* The Artist's Way *is a wonderful guide for excavating and appreciating your creativity. She counsels readers to set weekly* **artist's dates** *with themselves, just a half hour a week to explore your own creativity or the creativity of others.*

**FEEL FREE TO CHANGE.** Change is the cousin of courage. It takes some steam to say "I was *that,* and now I am *this.*" Change is not a sacrifice, it is essential to fully living. It's OK to let go, and it's marvelous to move forward. Change can be redeeming. Forget about what they might think at the office, and don't worry about whether your partner can keep up with you or not. Step forward into your life.

**PRACTICE.** *Consider how you've changed in the past year or over the years. And let it be known. Write out a change tally for yourself.* For example: Stopped caring so much about what the neighbors think; improved the energy of the living room by getting rid of that chair I never really liked; I now spend my money on experiences instead of stuff; I no longer tolerate criticism; I'm plenty more compassionate.

*Have a "How have we changed?" jam session with a good friend (this is an especially potent conversation to have with life partners). Talk about what you've outgrown and come to know and love and left behind. You may be amazed at who you've become.*

**WATCH FOR SIGNS.** Synchronicity is an indicator that you're on the right track. As our friend and philosopher Peter Russell puts it, "A characteristic of synchronicities is that they tend to support our needs. They seem to bring us just what we need, at just the right time. It is as if the Universe has my best interests at heart, and arranges for their fulfillment in ways which I could never have dreamt of." ("How to be a Wizard," www.peterrussell.com)

**PRACTICE.** *What has come to you easily or serendipitously? When do you feel blessed and most natural in your life? Conversely, when does it feel like you're fighting an uphill battle with cement in your shoes? Where do you encounter resistance or feel imprisoned? It's important in this part of the exercise to distinguish between the struggle that weighs you down and the struggle that you do with a glad heart.*

**BE RUTHLESSLY DISCERNING.** Bring into your life only what you love! Do not compromise. Think of your Style Statement as your personal bodyguard. Make sure you take it shopping with you to ward off impulse purchases and on-sale seductions.

**PRACTICE.** *Make a list of what you are inspired to say yes to and compelled to say no to in your life.*

# Life Walk-Through

If you weave the central and layered question, *"What is the spirit, look, and feel of my Style Statement?"* through the different domains of the **Lifestyle Map,** you will get a clearer view of your authentic self in action.

Think of this as a multidimensional checklist for the countless ways you can apply your Style Statement. These are not meant to serve as strict categories but, rather, as possible ways of expressing yourself.

## HOME + STUFF

What is the spirit, look, and feel of *(insert Style Statement)*?

Living space (house, condo, apartment): design type, era, culture, colors
Furnishings: style, materials, line, texture

Art and objects: themes, artists/craftspeople/designer, mediums, era
Appliances and technology: computer, entertainment system, kitchen aids

## FASHION + SENSUALITY

What is the spirit, look, and feel of *(insert Style Statement)*?

Casual wear: pants, tops, dresses, sweaters, outerwear

Business wear: pants, tops, dresses, suits, outerwear

Celebration wear: pants, tops, dresses, suits, outerwear

Accessories: shoes, boots, jewelry, flourishes, ties, wraps, belts, hats, eyewear

Colors: base and foundation colors, accent and impact colors

Silhouette: cuts, lines, flow, proportion

Hair: style, cut, color

Makeup: style, emphasis, colors, essential products and tools

Body art: tattoos, piercings

Scent: body, home

Sexuality: philosophy, frequency, style, atmosphere, character, connection

## SPIRIT + LEARNING

What is the spirit, look, and feel of *(insert Style Statement)?*

Philosophy: what is your personal, spiritual perspective?

Practice: reflective, engaged, meditative, formal, therapeutic, alone, in intimate relationships, with family, in group/community

Learning: audio, visual, kinesthetic, solitary, group/community

Education: experiential, formal study, short-term, long-term

## RELATIONSHIPS + COMMUNICATION

What is the spirit, look, and feel of *(insert Style Statement)?*

Self: free time, solitude, therapy, daily rituals

Friends and family: keeping in touch, mode of connecting, intention

Colleagues: interacting, leadership, follow-through

Tools for communicating: stationery, greeting cards, business cards, Web site, e-mail, blog, phone messages, gifts

## BODY + WELLNESS

What is the spirit, look and feel of *(insert Style Statement)?*

Nutrition: foods, beverages, supplements, tastes, cultures, preparation

Fitness: athletics, hobbies, activities, games, types of training

Feeling: corporal body, internal body, spiritual body

Prevention and healing: philosophy, modalities, training, remedies, practitioners

## SERVICE + WEALTH

What is the spirit, look, and feel of *(insert Style Statement)?*

Vocation: job, career, profession, creations, products, services

Presentation: image, networking, marketing, promise to deliver

Philanthropy: causes, issues, projects, communities, ways of contributing, volunteering, advising, tithing, donating

Money: earning, saving, spending, investing

## CREATIVITY + CELEBRATION

What is the spirit, look, and feel of *(insert Style Statement)?*

Creative expression: visual art, performance, writing, crafts, clothing, furnishings, home decor, landscape, cooking, problem solving, strategizing

Entertaining: get-togethers, dinner parties, holidays, gifts, settings, decor, entertainment, ambience, location, games, food, music, fashion

## NATURE + REST & RELAX

What is the spirit, look, and feel of *(insert Style Statement)?*

At the start of your day: waking up, ritual, prayer, thoughts, exercise.

When you need to recharge: time off, solitude, friends, entertainment

On holiday: location, culture, activities, people

Entertainment: theater, movies, music, reading, sports, socializing

# Go Forth and Live as Art!

*What if you looked your very best?*

*What if you felt at home wherever you went?*

*What if you became more of yourself every day?*

It is said that before they went into battle, some Indian warriors painted a butterfly symbol on their shields—not a growling wildcat or the buffalo horns we might expect to see in battle, but the image of a butterfly, the most delicate of creatures. Why? Because to be that tender and wet-winged, to break through the sturdy walls of a cocoon, and to fly into a world that is completely unknown is the ultimate act of bravery.

Authenticity is not for the faint of heart. To fly in the face of history, circumstance, and uncertainty, with your truth fully unfurled, takes some serious moxy. When you want to love and be loved (and what else is there, really?), your truth becomes a very tender thing, and sharing it is a mighty gift. So perhaps being genuine is an everyday act of heroism. To all the heart-dwelling heroes who dare to be precisely who they are, we applaud you!

Life is an invitation to live out loud, in color, in contrast to everything around you that is shellacked or shallow or sold in bulk. Bring your whole self to work. Paint the world with your opinions. Say yes! to your assets and your foibles. Get dressed up. Take pride in what you love. Cordially decline offers to conform. Be profoundly and completely you, and revel in the deep peace that such sincerity brings.

Shine.

*keep in touch,*
*Carrie + Danielle*

# Style Vocabulary+

# Foundation Words

These are ideal Foundation Words because they can be applied to the spirit, look, and feel of something— they work for both the material and the immaterial.

In our experience, these are the most common Foundation Words in people's Style Statements. In a sense, they are archetypal in their breadth and scope. They represent essential, fundamental truths for many people.

This list is by no means exhaustive. Feel free to venture out to find a better-fitting word if you don't click with any of these.

THIS CHART IS LOOSELY STRUCTURED. SOME OF THESE WORDS NATURALLY RELATE AND CLUSTER TOGETHER. FOR EXAMPLE, *CONTEMPORARY, MODERN,* AND *CURRENT* ARE CLEARLY RELATED IN NATURE, AS ARE *TRADITIONAL, TIMELESS,* AND *ENDURING.* SO YOU MIGHT FIND THAT CERTAIN "GROUPS" OF WORDS APPEAL TO YOU, AND RECOGNIZING THAT MIGHT HELP YOU CLARIFY WHAT THEMES ARE STRONGEST FOR YOU. THAT SAID, FEEL FREE TO CHOOSE WORDS FOR YOURSELF THAT ARE NOT NECESSARILY "RELATED" TO EACH OTHER HERE.

| | |
|---|---|
| *Contemporary* | *Constructed* *Constructive* |
| *Modern* *Modernist* | *Tailored* |
| *Current* | *Design* *Designed* *Designing* |
| *Bohemian* | *Creative* *Creatively* *Creativity* |
| *Bold* *Boldly* *Boldness* | *Harmonious* *Harmony* |

| | | | | |
|---|---|---|---|---|
| Composed | Elegance<br>Elegant<br>Elegantly | Cosmopolitan | Sophisticated<br>Sophistication | Classic<br>Classical |
| Structured | Cultivated<br>Cultivating | Refined | Traditional | Timeless |
| Innovative | Cultured<br>Cultural | Genteel<br>Gentility<br>Gentleman | Nostalgic | Enduring |
| Simple<br>Simplified<br>Simplistic<br>Simply | Grace<br>Graceful<br>Gracious | Feminine<br>or<br>Masculine | Rustic | Cherish<br>Cherished<br>Cherishing |
| Comfort<br>Comfortable<br>Comforting | Natural<br>Naturally | Sensual<br>Sensuality | Organic | Genuine<br>Genuinely |
| | Understated | Elemental | Essence<br>Essential | Sacred |

## Bohemian

**SPIRIT:** Bohemian is the ultimate champion and devotee of the arts, taking a stand for self-expression and creative liberty. Bohemian derives soul-deep satisfaction from generating their own creative momentum and helping others to be seen, heard, and rewarded for what they do. Bohemian adores the unconventional, quirky, avant-garde, and slightly or outra-geously offbeat. Truly, Bohemians have attitude fortitude! They put very little stock in what other people think of them, and when strict convention or pettiness encroaches, they rail with protest or hit the road without a second thought. Bucking the system makes them giddy with delight, but because they are so culturally in-formed and current, they can navigate with social ease whenever they wish. However, Bohemian can become prey to its own rebellious nature, and must consciously juggle self-determination with compassion. Bohemian is a free spirit, free thinker, a traveler of the world and of the mind.

**LOOK & FEEL:** Bohemian loves to be up-to-date with design and often combine what's current with an eclectic collection of art, trinkets, and keepsakes. Cultur-ally sophisticated: from high art to street punk. Wild, modern, edgy, offbeat, unconventional.

*avant-garde, beatnik, contemporary, cool, deep, eccentric, extremist, groovy, far-out, flower child, hippie, liberal,* *maverick, mod, modernistic, New Age traveler, nonconformist, original, out of this world, radical, way-out*

## Bold / Boldly / Boldness

**SPIRIT:** Bold has a strong warrior spirit that can translate into risk-taking, maverick ideas, and lively adventures. Go big, or go home. Do it right, or don't do it at all. That's Bold. Bold will automatically question established rules and set out to challenge whatever they perceive as unjust or sub-quality. They inquire; they look beneath the surface; they like to know the facts; they are wired to make an impact in whatever they do. They can be incredibly imaginative, and critical thinkers, and it's their ability to get out of the box that makes them great trend spotters and assessors of what's happening. Bold gravitates to people who can effect change, and can always identify a winning formula or the overachiever in the room. In over-drive, Bold can be aggressive or imperceptive, which might lead to isolation—a less-than-ideal circum-stance, because Bold prefers to be surrounded by people. They are quite comfortable with uncertainty because they know that they can draw on their own daring and multiple resources to fully embrace any situation. They are almost always sure that they've made the right choice. They focus forward. They take charge and persevere. Bold is sure to be noticed.

**LOOK & FEEL:** Bold likes unique designs, a bit of flare. Solid structures, strong shapes, generous and bountiful events, full sensory experiences. Outstanding, eye-catching, substantial.

*adventurous, assured, brave, challeng-ing, collected, confident, courageous, daring, dramatic, extensive, gallant, great, hearty, imaginative, intrepid, largesse, noticeable, poised, prominent, self-possessed, stubborn, trusting, valiant*

## Cherish / Cherished / Cherishing

**SPIRIT:** A collector of friends, experi-ences, and well-worn things; when Cherished loves you, you know it. Cherished is deeply sentimental, though not necessarily stuck in the past, because Cherished is always endeavoring to create new life experiences and memories. They love to celebrate, venture out, and bring good people and worthy causes together. Cherished adores hearing or telling a good story and have plenty of them to share. Natural and gleeful caretakers, Cherished has an abun-dance of nurturing energy and affection, which is generously given to strengthen and sustain. They can be generous to a fault and need to remember that they do not have to save the world—caring for themselves first and foremost is a great way to be of service. With an unshakable values system and moral compass, Cherished can be remarkably determined and focused. Love is its strength.

**LOOK & FEEL:** If there's a story behind it, it works for Cherished! Nostalgic, sentimental, culturally rich, and diverse. Personalized, attention to detail, inviting. Because Cherished can be both "in the moment" and "in the past," fashion and decor can be a combination of the simple and contemporary, vintage and Old World.

*admire, adore, appreciate, apprize, care for, comfort, cultivate, delight in, dote on, embrace, enshrine, entertain, fancy, foster, harbor, hold dear, honor, imagine, like, love, nature, nourish, nurture, preserve, prize, respect, revere, shelter, support, treasure, value, venerate, worship*

## Classic / Classical

**SPIRIT:** Classic chooses quality, lasting and enduring value, and experiences, people, and things from the highest rank or class. Classic is known and appreciated for being cordial, refined, and somewhat formal. They feel somewhat romantic about the past and often appreciate and respect tradition. Because they strive for excellence and perfection, they do their homework and practice due diligence. They are great at getting the most out of a system and will typically seek out authoritative advice and choose established or recognized standards rather than experimental or futuristic options. Their decisions are measured and certain. They have a sense of nobility, err on the side of convention, and take pride in their principles and values. The shadow side of Classic can be overly controlled or restrained. Classic loves to nurture and support things that will have lasting significance and value or the potential to create a legacy.

**LOOK & FEEL:** Classic goes for the best. Quality, top of its class, superior. Simplified and harmonious. Restrained, conservative, elegant. Having historical or legendary associations.

*Champion, class act, classy, conservative, controlled, decisive, definitive, enduring, ideal, immortal, perfectionist, polite, proper, timeless, time-honored, top-notch*

## Comfort / Comfortable / Comforting

**SPIRIT:** Comfortable is the consummate pleasure seeker. Physical comforts are paramount, and sensual gratification is a fundamental part of their lives. In their best form, Comfortable is easygoing, sincerely cheerful, and free from doubt. They can be highly sensitive, and when they feel something in their bones, they will operate with steady determination. When challenged, they will do what it takes to regain their equilibrium, whether that means escaping from a situation or facing it head-on. Comfortable is like a willow tree, flexible but deeply rooted. A peacekeeper and nurturer, Comfortable is welcoming and soothing and always makes time for socializing and celebration. They strive to put those around them at ease, so they are often fabulous hosts—they love to please and accommodate. Sometimes getting out of their "comfort zone" makes it difficult for them to make a change, take a leap, or trust wholeheartedly. Nest eggs, backup plans, something to fall back on—Comfortable tend to be focused on security, whether financial or familial or emotional, and will naturally strive to preserve it. Comfortable is a generous spirit.

Look & Feel: Comfortable is body centered, so the priority with fashion and furnishings is comfort. Casual, plush, overstuffed, loose-fitting, durable; warm tones; earthy; sensual rich textures; sentimental, romantic, nostalgic, luxurious, roomy, convenient, cozy, charming, spacious, airy.

*agreeable, ample, appropriate, cared for, cheerful, convenient, cushy, delightful, easy, happy, healthy, hearty, made well, pleasant, pleased, protected, relaxing, restful, restored, rich, roomy, satisfying, serene, soft, strengthened, useful, well-off*

## Composed

**SPIRIT:** Composed aspires to successfully integrate body, mind, and spirit. Composed is arranged, poised, gracious, and refined. They love to create order and ease for themselves or for others, whether in physical space and surroundings or in operational solutions and systems. Composed is always steadily and calmly pulling together things, people, and their own thoughts and emotions. They prefer well-managed time, tidy spaces, and healthy, compartmentalized feelings. Inner peace and feeling "at home" are synonymous to them. Ideally, their home or work space is a temple, a sanctuary that allows for reflection, relaxation, and serenity. When stretched, Composed may become fixated on details or generate a false sense of security. Practical and pragmatic, yet often creatively inclined, Composed thrives on artistic expression or active appreciation of the arts. Composed innately strives for balance, from which comes strength, confidence, resolve, and moxie.

**LOOK & FEEL**: Put together, coordinated, structured, organized, staged, laid out, calming, soothing, peaceful, tranquil. Can range from contemporary and modern to holistically influenced simplicity.

*arranged, assertive, build, calm, clearheaded, collect, comfort, compound, comprise, confident, construct, control, distill, ease, fashion, Feng Shui, form, make, merge, moderate, modulate, organize, pacify, quiet, recollect, reconcile, regulate, relax, repress, resolve, restrain, sensible, self-assured, settled, simplify, soften, solace, staged, tempered, Zen*

## Constructed / Constructive

**SPIRIT**: Constructive love rhythm, order, patterns, circuitry, cohesiveness, fine-tuning, and all roads that lead to harmony. They are a wonderful combination of pragmatism and warmth. They love the interplay of experiences and qualities and memories that build on each other to form relationships. Making things happen, creating results, and being clearly expressive are all core motivators for Constructive. Whether it's an improved system, a work of art, or a dinner party, Constructive must keep things moving in the right direction—and usually have a precise way of getting there. They need a sound foundation of love or ritual in their lives, or a sense of disconnectedness or worry can creep in. Support systems are key to their well-being and productivity. Constructive can be a forgiving friend or partner and are of strong and generous character, always facing up to life and making the most of what they have to work with.

**LOOK & FEEL**: Sturdy, complex, detailed, strategic, systematic; rhythmical beats, patterns, graphics; strong shapes, bold colors; highly contoured, architectural, tailored elements; socially responsible manufacturing and production.

*adorning, advancing, artistic, beautifying, beneficial, broadening, complete, crafted, designed, developmental, disciplining, educational, effective, elevating, enlightening, ennobling, enriching, expanding, helpful, humane, influential, innovative, inspirational, instructive, liberal, nurturing, positive, practical, productive, refined, regenerative, socializing, stimulating, structured, tailored, timely, uplifting, useful, valuable, virtual, wholesome*

## Contemporary

**SPIRIT**: Contemporary has a strong presence, because they are indeed "present." Contemporary looks you in the eye. They are up-to-date and current with what matters most to them and are typically interested in social and cultural issues. They stay on top of things; they make time work for them; they look to the future. Progressive thinkers, they seek out leading-edge ideas and people to help them get where they want to go. Contemporary is often champion of a cause. They prefer to interact with genuine and authentic people but can tolerate many types of personalities in order to achieve their goals, from having a good time to purpose-driven missions. In overdrive, Contemporary can be forceful or critical, especially of themselves and their healthy limitations. Living from a place of inspiration and always curious, Contemporary turns possibility into real time, with pragmatism, common sense, and a clarity of commitment.

**LOOK & FEEL**: Modern; in style but not necessarily trendy; potentially avant-garde; clean, new, well-cared for. Simple lines; open spaces and surfaces.

*abreast, au courant, connected, current, in fashion, informed, in touch, in style, latest, leading edge, linked, modern, new, now, present, present-day, recent, synchronous, topical, up-to-date*

## Cosmopolitan

**SPIRIT:** Cosmopolitan thrives on new experiences, sights, sounds, and cultures. Curious and adventurous, they consider the planet their playground and will go well out of their way for a taste of it, even if that means traveling to far-flung cultures and places. Cosmopolitan has wanderlust and, whether in a library, at a conference, or on the Internet, naturally seek out new ideas and connections. Innately attracted to unique, odd, or exotic things and people, Cosmopolitan has a marvelous collection of diverse friends. Because of their many rich life experiences, they tend to be liberal, progressive, and enlightened thinkers, often advocating for change, improvement, or reform, and willing to experiment. In excess, they might push for change merely for the sake of change or flee when they should stay and fight. Penultimate city lovers, Cosmopolitan adores a great dinner party, art opening, fashion show, or concert, and love to engage on world issues and wisdom.

**LOOK & FEEL:** Sophisticated, citified, hip, exotic, unique, textured, current, global, polished, present-day. Cosmopolitans are often eclectic, a touch dramatic, and can pull off both high fashion and bohemian.

*advanced, adept, artistry, clever, connected, cultivated, current, craftsmanship, flexible, freethinking, global, gregarious, indulgent, in fashion, instant, liberal, metropolitan, open, permissive, polished, present, progressive, public, radical, responsive, smooth, sophisticated, tolerant, topical, unbiased, unbigoted, undogmatic, universal, urbane, worldly-wise*

## Creative / Creatively / Creativity

**SPIRIT:** Creative is a life-affirming explorer. Gifted with fantastic imaginations, Creative will seek out originality—unique people and experiences, abstract thinking, and fantastical, whimsical notions. Small-mindedness and regulation deeply pains Creative. Resourceful, determined, and passionate, they can find a way through any circumstance. Naturally flexible and positively capable of reinventing themselves and turning situations around, they tend to be comfortable with change. Fully expressed, Creative is a powerful force that can inspire people to change for the better or to shift directions. They are highly sensitive to their surroundings and, for better or worse, can be sponges for emotions and information. They feel most useful when they are being inspired or inspiring others. They live to express themselves in their own way. On a dark day, they feel disconnected from their source of inspiration—whether it be material or immaterial, earthly or divine—adrift or on the "outside" of things. In the best of times, Creative feels a deep sense of harmony and synchronicity with positive forces that keep life moving forward. Creative endeavors to respect others' forms of expression and can be very tolerant.

**LOOK & FEEL:** Original, unique, one-of-a-kind. Crafted, innovative, colorful, abstract, thought-out, free-flowing, artistic. Creative always put things together in their own way.

*aesthetic, artistic, clever, cool, crafty, cultivated, cultured, dramatic, elegant, exquisite, fertile, formative, gifted, graceful, grand, harmonious, hip, ideal, imaginative, ingenious, innovative, inspired, inventive, musical, original, ornamental, pictorial, picturesque, pleasing, poetic, productive, prolific, refined, rhythmical, satisfying, sensitive, skillful, stimulating, stylish, sublime, talented, tasteful, visionary*

## Cultivated / Cultivating

**SPIRIT:** Cultivated takes tremendous pleasure in seeing things grow. They love to nurture their inner life, other people, animals, nature, and ultimately good ideas. Happy to foster and promote the growth of others, Cultivated works toward what is best for the individual as well as the group. They are interesting to other people precisely because they are actively and sincerely interested in the world around them. They respect, honor, and celebrate the customs of various communities and traditions and are consummate connectors of people. They are natural leaders. Positively passionate about growing, learning, and teaching, Cultivated is often well trained or educated (either formally or self-taught) and thus can sometimes be quite self-critical, overextending for accomplishments. They always have some pursuit or exploration under way. Cultivated considers all of life's experiences—positive and negative—nutrients for the inner garden from which they reap their harvest.

**LOOK & FEEL:** Always quality, with a high degree of taste. Can run the gamut from sophisticated and refined to culturally diverse, eccentric, or bohemian. Rich, artistic, intellectually advanced. Full range of textures, tastes, and aromas.

*able, adept, aestheticism, art, brainy, civilization, class, consummate, cool, delicacy, dignity, discrimination, dress, education, elegance, elevation, enlightenment, experience, expert, fashion, finish, gentility, gifted, good taste, grace, hip, improvement, kindness, learning, manners, masterly, nobility, perception, polished, practiced, proficient, refinement, savoir faire, savvy, sharp, skillful, sophistication, tact, talented, training, urbanity, wised up, with it*

## Cultured / Cultural

**SPIRIT:** The life of Cultured is a mosaic of experiences, beliefs, and aspirations. They are keenly interested in the practices, policies, and sensibilities of other groups and cultures. They love to know how other people live and work, strive and succeed. They are curious about the origins of ideas,

motivations of people, and sources of products and materials. Cultured is the master of "think global, act local." While they're always open to outside sources of wisdom and advice, ultimately they rely heavily on their own life experiences and knowledge. To a large extent, their commitment to honor and to create diversity defines them, though sometimes their tolerance and political correctness can keep them from stepping out of bounds and freely expressing themselves. Cultured is a great listener who is always paying attention to what's going on—in the world at large, in the local community, and in close relationships—and derive deep pleasure in sharing helpful findings and contributing to important conversations and endeavors.

**LOOK & FEEL:** Polished and respectful. Somewhat dignified and classy. Refined manners. Well traveled. Mosaics, patchworks, tapestries. Primitive and tribal work. Storytelling, legends, a sense of history.

*aestheticism, art, civilization, class, customs, delicacy, development, dignity, discrimination, dress, education, elegance, elevation, enlightenment, ethnology, experience, fashion, finish, folklore, folkways, gentility, good taste, grace, grounding, habit, humanism, ideas, kindness, knowledge, learning, lifestyle, manners, perception, polish, refinement, savoir faire, society, sophistication, training, urbanity*

## Current

**SPIRIT:** Current is intensely energetic, electrical, moving, and steadily flowing, and often acts as a channel or conductor for multidimensional energy. Their hearts' desire is to connect with the divine and to bring that radiance forward to enhance and enliven others. Artistically and creatively gifted, they very naturally find a way to express their deepest nature and desires. They thrive on exchanges of ideas and concepts and on interactions in commerce or with other people. They are incredibly engaging, often generous to a fault, and talkative. They love to be the center of attention and are at ease with admirers and adulation. They often seem to have an endless supply of energy. In excess, Current can become zealous or righteous and have a tendency to over-spiritualize or over-intellectualize. Always moving forward, Current is a progressive, modern thinker, liberal to proudly radical, up-to-date and topical in their views and opinions.

**LOOK & FEEL:** Modern, contemporary, new, in fashion, hip, avant-garde. Currents are health and eco-conscious and aspire to purity. Organic, uninterrupted clean lines, simplified, vibrant, well-lit. Relevant and essential, pared down.

*activity, airflow, channel, charged, circulating, contemporary, energy, enlightened, electricity, fashionable, force, hip, inspiration, instant, intensity, in vogue, modern, now, ongoing, popular, present, prevailing, ruling, topical, up-to-date, widespread, zephyr*

## Design / Designed / Designing

**SPIRIT:** Designed absolutely, positively adores simplicity and things that "make the most sense." They applaud original thinking and effective systems and are innately innovative, inventive, strategic, and intentional. Designed loves to know what the plan is or to improve on it. In pursuit of solutions or creativity, Designed can be an excellent researcher, networker, brainstormer, and visionary. They seek out contemporaries and modernizers to nourish their spirit and intellect. On a bad day, Designed can be overly willful or get stuck on the details of a strategy. They strive for mastery and excellence in focused areas. Visual expression is frequently of utmost importance to Designed. They are sincerely open to new ideas and ways of doing things, yet confident in their own perspectives and opinions. Designed dispenses advice when asked but does so with tremendous consideration and restraint.

**LOOK & FEEL:** Modern, contemporary; could be futuristic. Tailored, custom-made, architectural. Designed loves patterns, graphics, icons, simplified complexity, and symbols. Appreciate state-of-the-art, handcrafted, and efficient construction.

*architectural, built, contemplated, creative, constructed, custom-made, deliberate, examined, expressed, innovated, intentional, invented, investigated, mediated, mindful, navigated, planning, purposeful, reasoned, schematic, strategic, studied, studious, thought out, tailored, treated, weighed, well-advised, well cut, willful*

## Elegance / Elegant / Elegantly

**SPIRIT:** Elegant is a class act: poised, gracious, respectful. Presentation matters to them. Elegant very much cares how it all comes together—outfits, business plans, and celebrations. The truly Elegant are masters of restraint and humbly respectful. They are never over the top and certainly never skimp. Elegant knows when to look away or to be silent, and seek to lend dignity and honor to all situations. They are direct without being forceful. Elegant prizes solutions and are driven to find the optimal way of achieving a goal, usually through a method ineffably simple and precise. They create power with simplicity. They delight in being exact, and they always seem to get things just right. When they feel stressed or derided, they can withdraw abruptly or turn sharp and critical in defense. Elegant pays attention to the details, ever so tenderly, and zealously avoids what is crass or lacking in integrity.

**LOOK & FEEL:** Elegant moves with grace. Uncomplicated. Sleek. Refined. Mature. Attention to detail. Great posture. Gentle, poised, composed, graceful. Put together, refreshed. Tasteful opulence. Can be ornate but harmonious.

*appropriate, apt, artistic, balance, beauty, charm, clarity, class, classic, choice, cultivation, culture, delicacy, dignity, discernment, distinction, effective, exquisiteness, gentility, good, grace, grandeur, ingenious, lushness, luxury, magnificence, polish, purity, refinement, restraint, rhythm, simplicity, sophistication, splendor, stylized, sumptuousness, symmetry, tastefulness*

## Elemental

**SPIRIT:** Elemental is interested in the underlying forces of life: what inspires and moves people, the miracle and majesty of nature, the machinations of science and engineering, the mysteries of the universe. They love to unearth the guiding theme or architecture of things, and if answers and origins can't be found, they will devise their own theories and stories. Fantastical, ethereal, gossamer, fluid, and having a mischievous sense of humor, Elemental is a dreamer who loves to bring the magical into everyday life. They often find themselves at the intersection of art and science. They are incredibly adept at juggling logic and faith, gentleness and passion, fluidity and force. They can easily go off on tangents and may become untethered from practicalities. Balance is critical to their success on all levels. They love to roam and explore, so they usually feel at home wherever they are. They relish good conversation about the divine, physics, psychology, and cultural tides. They are philosophers at heart and need creative outlets to wonder aloud and express their perceptions of the world.

**LOOK & FEEL:** Natural textiles, organic, earthy, rustic. Peasant. Beautiful imperfections. Gossamer, flowing, draped, wrapped. Linen, raw silk, felt, cottons, suede. Relating to or resembling the forces of nature.

*animate, basic, cellular, central, compelling, dynamic, effective, energetic, essential, fundamental, graceful, indigenous, indispensable, ingrained, inherent, instinctive, integral, intrinsic, key, living, main, natural, necessary, organic, potent, primary, primitive, principal, radical, strong, underlying, vigorous, vital*

### Enduring

**SPIRIT:** Tough cookies, rugged, unwavering, devoted, and ultimately pragmatic, Enduring is profoundly patient and can stay the course with a steady heart and mind. Whether socially conventional or rebellious, Enduring has a great sense of dignity, pride, and principles. When Enduring commits, they do so wholeheartedly and with certainty. Never one to back down from adversity or conflict, Enduring stands up to support friends, mates, and chosen causes. Leaders and stewards of ideas,

Enduring can be equally effective and at ease in a team or independently. The shadow side of Enduring is unyielding stubbornness and a tendency to suffer or tolerate "too much" without out taking positive action. Enduring generously gives and openly receives acknowledgment and recognition.

**LOOK & FEEL:** The spectrum of Enduring ranges from timeless pieces drawn from ancient cultures and classic tradition to street-smart and rugged. Solid, durable, tightly woven, heavy-duty textiles; chunky, sturdy, dark, bold, storytelling.

*abiding, constant, continuing, everlasting, fast, firm, indestructible, lasting, permanent, persistent, persisting, stable, steadfast, steady, strong, tenacious, timeless, tough, traditional, unchanging*

### Essence / Essential

**SPIRIT:** Essence is guided by a determined search for what is divine and pure. Essence truly and deeply relishes the journey of life and trusts that the destination is momentary and perfect. The penultimate idealists, Essence leans toward the positive and puts things in the best light possible. They steward causes, rally for hope, and respond generously to the needs of others. They play by their own rules of reason—what matters most to Essence is the connection with the hearts of others and with natural forces. These sacred priorities keep them playful and

spontaneous and help them to transcend the mundane and to stay true to their vision of fulfillment. On a dark day, they can become overwhelmed by the span and depth of their own emotion. Practical work—chop wood; carry water—helps to clear their minds and regrounds them. Essence gets to the heart of the matter, with graceful precision. They have the capacity to move mountains with their single-mindedness and conviction.

**LOOK & FEEL:** Essence of plants and minerals, natural materials, pure colors. Lean toward simplistic, graceful design. Uncomplicated. Purified. Rarity, original.

*absolute, capital, cardinal, chief, constitutional, crucial, deep-seated, elemental, elementary, foremost, fundamental, ideal, imperative, important, indispensable, inherent, innate, intrinsic, key, leading, main, material, necessary, perfect, primary, prime, primitive, principal, pure, quintessential, required, requisite, underlying, vital, wanted*

### Feminine / Femininity

**SPIRIT:** Feminine is a force to be reckoned with—sheer womanpower. They are nurturing, inclusive, and intrinsically and actively compassionate. Midwives and caretakers of ideas and community, Feminine is often sought out for guidance, inspiration, and comfort. In full bloom, she has a great sense of adventure, as well as a healthy balance of responsibility. Feminine regularly exercises her prerogative to change her mind, start over, or wait it out. Sometimes Feminine can struggle with excessive or repressed emotion, thereby denying herself and those around her the full richness of her significant power. Feminine's holistic, often metaphysical perspective on life honors spirituality as the key to fulfillment. By far, Feminine's greatest gift is her intuition. Her ability to sense the truth of what's happening or what is to come is an incredibly effective tool for creating desirable realities.

**LOOK & FEEL:** All things woman: shapeliness, curves, softness. Sumptuous, luxurious, generous, comfortable, fluid. Tends to be ornate or artistic. Florals, flourish, color. Light, sparkling, radiance.

*changeable, charming, delicate, effete, empathetic, fair, fertile, gentle, girly, goddess, graceful, intuitive, ladylike, maidenly, mama, pure, queen, refined, sensitive, sexy, shy, soft, tender, twisty, vixen, womanly, yin*

## Genteel / Gentility

**SPIRIT:** Genteel is the ultimate lady. Quietly powerful, she is poised, dignified, and well mannered. She may speak softly, but Genteel's words are chosen very mindfully and purposefully—her ethics and morals are as strong as her loving heart. Genteel feels a great sense of devotion to her family and heritage. She is a natural healer. She loves to foster ideas and to develop and implement the most elegant and sensible way of doing things. She prefers to know as much as she possibly can about what interests her. Genteel is an excellent hostess and loves to give and receive gifts. When she is out of sync with her own inner voice, Genteel may become overly accommodating and silent or confined by her own rules. But it is the combination of sensitivity and dignified poise that makes for her resolute character. Genteel's forms of feminine power can range from honoring traditions to enterprising, women-based solutions to freedom of sexual expression.

**LOOK & FEEL:** Undeniably feminine, sophisticated, sensual, calm, gentle. Sacred objects, tranquil sanctuaries, and places of devotion. Proper manners and traditional celebrations. Often appreciates flowing, graceful materials. Loves lingerie.

*aristocratic, civil, courteous, courtly, cultivated, cultured, distinguished, elegant, fashionable, formal, graceful, intellectual, knowledgeable, ladylike, mannered, noble, ostentatious, polished, polite, precious, refined, respectable, romantic, sensitive, straitlaced, stylish, understanding*

## Gentleman / Gentlemanly

Spirit: Gentleman is a truly charming combination of warmth and strength, sincerity and nonchalance. He wears his power modestly, and though he may abide by standards and traditions, he is fully aware how persuasive and affecting thoughtfulness can be—in matters of the heart and in business. He loves to shepherd ideas into form, dispense information and wisdom, and develop and implement the best course of action to get things accomplished. Gentleman is instinctively protective and will go out of the way to demonstrate his devotion to people and projects. He feels great fidelity to his family and heritage. If he loses touch with his natural instincts, Gentleman may withdraw and become overly accommodating or confined by his own rules and principles. Liberal but genuine with his compliments, and a touch old-fashioned but entirely contemporary, he prefers to know as much as he possibly can about that which interests him.

**LOOK & FEEL:** Undeniably masculine, sophisticated, sensual, calming, warm. Symbolic objects, comforting home base, and energizing getaways. Proper manners and traditional celebrations. Often appreciate handcrafted, well-engineered, and timeless works.

*admirer, aristocratic, cavalier, civilized, courteous, courtly, cultivated, cultured, distinguished, elegant, fashionable, formal, intellectual, intolerant, knowledgeable, main man, manly, noble, ostentatious, polished, polite, precious, refined, respectable, romantic, sensitive, straitlaced, stylish, suitor, understanding, well-mannered,*

## Genuine / Genuinely

**SPIRIT:** Authentic and real, Genuine wants to be fully itself and deeply appreciate people and experiences that are free of hypocrisy or dishonesty. Sincerity is sweet music to their souls. They gravitate to those who are down-to-earth and unpretentious. They are expert at sensing the discomfort and needs of others and excel at putting people at ease, drawing on their humor, good manners, or tenderness to do so. Genuine has a knack for taking the best and leaving the rest. They want the facts. They rarely suffer fools, and they don't make much time for situations that go against their grain or distract them from their goals. It's fairly easy for them to walk away from situations that aren't serving them. Genuines' motto tends to be "Live and live." Ironically, Genuine can struggle with balancing its outer image with its inner desires and, for better or worse, will fake it to make it. They have a special fondness for originality and appreciate things that last and endure as well as people and principles that have stood the test of time.

**LOOK & FEEL:** Comfortable and comforting. Strong craftsmanship, standing the test of time. Almost anything goes with Genuines' fashion as long as it feels right. Genuine adores tried-and-true brands and things, and places and people steeped

with history and character. Replicas, rip-offs, and imitation designs and materials are out of the question.

*absolute, accurate, actual, authentic, bona fide, candid, certain, certified, conclusive, demonstrable, exact, factual, for real, good, hard, honest, honest-to-goodness, indubitable, legitimate, literal, natural, official, original, palpable, plain, positive, precise, proved, pure, real, sound, sterling, sure, tested, true, unadulterated, unalloyed, undoubted, unimpeachable, unquestionable, unvarnished, up-front, valid, veritable, very, whole*

## Grace / Graceful / Gracious

**SPIRIT:** Greek mythology tells of sister goddesses of joy, charm, and beauty called the three Graces. Graceful is poised and dignified and, at her best, is a giving, generous spirit who seeks to impart kindness and dignity. Love is her fuel; goodwill is her motivation and guide. Graceful prefers meaning and substance but will practice courtesy and compassion rather than forcing her views about a situation. Graceful has a sense of fit and propriety, a craving for balance and good form and proportion. She adores harmony and material and immaterial luxury—from finery to leisure. Rooted in feminine power, Graceful has a quiet and steady confidence. She endeavors to make everything special in the most considerate and ultimately charming ways, and she tends to make it all look effortless.

**LOOK & FEEL:** Adroitness, agility, allure, attractiveness, balance, beauty, cleanliness, ease, elegance. The proper fit and hang. Flow, warmth, comfort, harmony. Shapeliness, smoothness, style, suppleness, symmetry.

*attentive, benefaction, blessing, breeding, caritas, charity, compassion, consideration, cultivation, decency, dignity, divinity, etiquette, favor, finesse, finish, forgiveness, form, friendly, generosity, goodwill, invocation, kindness, love, mercy, poise, polish, prayer, propriety, tact, tastefulness, thanksgiving, royalty*

## Harmonious / Harmony

**SPIRIT:** Harmony is a jovial peacekeeper, the playful, dynamic cousin of grace and composure. Harmony fundamentally loves people and thrives on figuring out what makes them tick and how to get them to groove in concert. They can make an occasion out of good news and bring a sense of celebration to everything, usually uplifting an environment with their presence. Consummate team players, Harmony goes where they are needed. Working behind the scenes or as head coaches, they will do what it takes to get a job done. Not fond of loose ends, Harmony has the wherewithal to see things through to their conclusion. When their instinctive peace-keeping nature turns to placating and pleasing, Harmony is out of tune with itself. In attempting to keep everyone happy, Harmony can lose touch with its own genuine desires. A sense of place and ease is very important to Harmony. They are diligent about staying in touch, creating rich and vital living and work spaces, and making time for rest and relaxation.

**LOOK & FEEL:** Simplified, balanced, clean, flowing. Graceful, elegant, refined. Comfort. Peaceful. Musical. Rhythmical. Steady. Complementary: everything works well together.

*accord, affinity, agreement, amicability, combination, comfort, compatibility, concord, conformity, consensus, consistency, cooperation, correspondence, diplomat, ease, empathy, flow, friendship, grace, goodwill, home, kinship, like-mindedness, melody, pacifist, peace, progressive, rapport, statesman, sympathy, tranquility, understanding, unity*

## Innovative

**SPIRIT:** Consummate entrepreneurs, Innovative is always on the lookout for the next big thing, a breakthrough idea, or an invention. Innovative is forever seeking ways to renew, recharge, and replenish, and has a hard time with stagnation and unyieldingness. Perceptive, in tune, and extraordinarily resourceful, Innovative has a knack for finding and creating opportunities that lead to prosperity in multiple ways. They are connectors, mavens, and enthusiastic and natural networkers who make things happen. But Innovative has a tendency to rush ahead or be dismis-

sive of thoughts and experiences before they have been thoroughly explored. And with so many ideas to pursue, they can take on too much. They have a fascination with eccentric people and certainly have a few of their own quirks and eccentricities. They are unabashedly insatiable and determined. Fabulous cheerleaders and champions, Innovative adores being adored and blossoms with acknowledgement and adulation.

**LOOK & FEEL:** Unique, individualized, avant-garde, creative, cutting edge. Can range from high concept and highly stylized to quirky and whimsical. Custom-made and tailored. Typically simple and streamlined.

*artistic, avant-garde, clever, contemporary, creative, cutting edge, experimental, far-out, formative, imaginative, ingenious, inventive, leading edge, liberal, new, original, productive, prolific, radical, ready, resourceful, shrewd, stimulating, state-of-the-art, unconventional, visionary*

## Masculine

**SPIRIT:** Masculine is manpower. Confident and noble in character, his convictions are strong. He has a deep and determined sense of responsibility that is revealed in service to his family, friends, and community or through his vocation. Masculine is a protector of people, values, and concepts. Whether physically, psychologically, or spiritually, Masculine is a bold, brave,

and courageous spirit. If unbalanced, he can be overly aggressive or insensitive. He prizes accomplishment, achievements, and productivity. He puts things into motion and gets things done, as a leader and team player, maverick, and keeper of tradition. Masculine energy travels like an arrow to the bull's-eye: focused, intentional, and determined.

**LOOK & FEEL:** Strong shapes, durability, dark, rich, earthy, generous, practical, regal. Tend to be structured, constructed, sturdy.

*adult, bold, brave, brotherly, coach, comrade, fatherly, gallant, generative, guide, hardy, honorable, hunk, jock, leader, macho, male, manful, manly, mannish, muscular, potent, powerful, red-blooded, resolute, robust, supportive, stallion, stouthearted, strapping, strong, vigorous, virile, yang, winner*

## Modern / Modernist

**SPIRIT:** Modern is an idealist and visionary. They are aware of what's been popular or effective throughout generations, cultures, and industries. They predict change; they follow change; and they revere the innovators who have come before them. They are attracted to what works. Modern believes that the greatest concepts, designs, and theories are timeless and thus aspires to have or make things that are current and relevant but that will be useful and enduring. They like to have an impact. They want to be in style and in sync with what's happening and get anxious if they fall out of the loop or out of touch with what's going on—on personal and social levels—and can become a bit preoccupied with what's cool. Modern strives to be at the top of their game. They are pragmatic risk takers, calculating but capable of taking an unexpected turn if they see something appealing and potentially wonderful in the distance.

**LOOK & FEEL:** Avant-garde, metropolitan, contemporary, clean, streamlined; more negative space than positive space. Unique, a bit edgy, noticeable.

*current, cutting edge, elegant, exclusive, fresh, hip, latest, leading edge, neoteric, new-fashioned, novel, now, present, prevailing, recent, sharp, stylish, twentieth-century, up-to-date*

### Natural / Naturally

**SPIRIT:** Natural is genuine, free from artificiality, affectation, and inhibitions. Natural is known for being spontaneous and easygoing. Natural hates to be fenced in and riles against conformity and unreasonable rules, though they are rooted in moral certainty and a strong sense of justice. Very much at ease with their essential selves, Natural is often very instinctive, sensuous, or highly sexual. They aren't strangers to hedonism or pleasure seeking. They love to get down to basics and can be graceful and direct communicators. Down to

earth, literally and figuratively, Natural has a deep reverence and respect for nature and ecological systems, which delights and replenishes them, and an appreciation of supernatural forces.

**LOOK & FEEL:** All things generated by nature: wood, minerals, gems. Natural coloring, textiles, and produce. Rustic, primitive, flowing, native, or common to its surroundings.

*being oneself, candid, childlike, direct, easy, elemental, folksy, forthright, frank, genuine, green, handcrafted, homey, impulsive, innocent, instinctive, laid-back, leather, minerals, native, open, organic, plain, primitive, provincial, pure, raw, real, rustic, simple, simple-hearted, sincere, spontaneous, straightforward, trusting, unassuming, uncontrived, unpolished, unpretentious, up-front, untamed, wilderness, woodsy, wild*

### Nostalgic

**SPIRIT:** Nostalgic is an ambassador of sentiment. They collect memories, trinkets, rare and precious things, and memorabilia. Nostalgic loves to pay homage to what has gone before. Enamored by the past—from royalty to rock stars, family heirlooms to classic films—they work it into the present with charm, quirkiness, and often elegance. They are usually hopeful romantics, yearning and working toward creating fulfilling connections. Their social circle is very important to them, as are the basic social graces of

politeness and a welcoming heart. Nostalgic likes to look good. They put creative thought into their home and appearance and love trying their treasures and good finds together with contemporary basics. Their bittersweet yearning for the past or fantasized future can lead to melancholy, the cure for which is resolute trust and practical planning. Attracted to the whimsical and the precious, Nostalgic has a great eye and heart for detail and seeks to fill life with the small pleasures that matter most.

**LOOK & FEEL:** Vintage, antique, rarities, collectibles. Gentility, sweetness, poise. Romantic, dreamy, cinematic, glamorous.

*ancestry, culture, customs, enchanting, estate, fairy tale, fashion, fondness, heirloom, history, idealistic, imaginary, inheritance, legacy, mysterious, mythology, novel, passionate, picturesque, poetic, remembering, ritual, sentimental, tradition, wisdom*

### Organic

**SPIRIT:** Organic is a divine dichotomy: practical but spontaneous, structured but flowing. The disposition of Organic is like that of bamboo—light, incredibly strong, growing freely and prolifically. Organic is mindful of the connections between parts, whether in relationships, systems, or physical things. They keenly sense what's going on (never miss a thing!) and what needs to happen in order to create harmony and ease—

Organic strives to unify. They are commonsensical, practical, and organized, and adore systems and solutions that simplify or create ease and efficiency. The challenge for Organic is to accept change without overthinking it, to trust what they already know is true. Organic is wholesome with pure intentions. Their feet are on the ground, and they are in tune with the natural order, seasons, and stages of living and working.

**LOOK & FEEL:** Organic's aesthetic is based on sensuality, quality, and construction—whether structured or flowing, shape is important. Timeless or simplistic styles, and handcrafted, socially responsible or eco-friendly materials. Layered aromas, rich textures, enduring and natural fabrics and substances; hearty and sturdy; never static, always changing; free from manufacturing, over-processing, and chemicals. Pure, essential, enduring.

*animate, basic, biological, cellular, constitutional, elemental, essential, fundamental, inherent, innate, integral, living, natural, necessary, original, primary, primitive, principal, structural, vital*

## Refined

**SPIRIT:** Refined is dignified, at ease, well mannered, and a touch old-fashioned. Good taste is at the top of their list. Refined is intentional and prefers to strategize, review things, and have a plan. Punctuality is a must, and precision is the intention. Refined

likes to redesign, reorganize, replenish, purify, perfect, polish, refine. They are self-assured, and no matter the circumstances emanate class and dignity, usually suggesting ease or wealth—in spirit or materially. They strive for purity—in food, behavior, colors, and surroundings—and avoid things that are distasteful, tacky, rugged, and crude. On a bad day, Refined can be slightly prudish or snooty. They appreciate a sense of history, thoughtful presentation, and values-based living. They aim for impeccability and don't waste time or energy on things or situations that are below their level of idealism and quality, though they will always decline or depart in the most gracious way possible.

**LOOK & FEEL:** Polished, poised, put together. Sophisticated, classic, traditional, elegant; clean lines, from crisp and tailored to graceful and fluid. Ranges from old world to contemporary design. Smooth, not coarse. Purified, refined materials. Also organic materials, raw minerals, polished finishes.

*aesthetic, civilized, clarified, clean, courteous, courtly, cultivated, delicate, discriminating, elegant, enlightened, exact, fastidious, finespun, genteel, gentlemanly, gracious, highbrow, high-minded, polished, polite, precise, proper, purified, rarefied, restrained, sensitive, snazzy, sophisticated, suave, sublime, subtle, tasteful, urbane, well-mannered*

## Rustic

**SPIRIT:** Rustic is the salt of the earth and as genuine as the day is long. Warmhearted, devoted, and loyal, they place family at the center of their lives. They invest their resources close to home and weave a close-knit circle of friends, relishing the strength and vitality of their own community, as well as others they visit in their travels. With their feet planted firmly on the ground, Rustic is a no-nonsense decision maker who is in it for the long haul. Their bounty is homegrown and handmade. Domesticity and nesting are their forte. Sometimes they can become too settled and need to push themselves to venture beyond familiar territory—both emotionally and physically—to keep learning and truly growing. Incredibly nurturing and supportive, Rustic is the friend who shows up to help hold down the fort, fix what's broken, or offer some old-fashioned tender loving care. They adore tradition, holidays, and any reason to bring good people together. Rustic enjoys tranquility when they find it, but fully embrace the beauty and richness of sometimes chaotic, full living.

**LOOK & FEEL:** Country, rural, small town. Homespun, handmade; craftsmanship. Roughly finished woods, textured appearances; heavy textiles and materials like stone and wrought iron. Earth tones, terra cottas. Natural. Charmingly simple.

*agrarian, agricultural, austere, bucolic, charming, countrified, homespun, homey, honest, natural, pastoral, picturesque, plain, pleasing, primitive, rural, simple, sylvan, unaffected, unpolished, unrefined, unsophisticated, verdant*

## Sacred

**SPIRIT:** Sacred is philosophically and theologically curious, perpetually searching for or creating meaning. They are habitually reflective, looking for divine synchronicities and lessons in everything. Often the one to initiate change, whether that be a promising beginning or a necessary end, Sacred walks a fine line between ruthless discrimination and tremendous tolerance. Advisers, mavens, and teachers, they reliably appear at the scene of life's big passages and events to bring grace and wit. Sacred loves to mark moments of insight and progress with celebrations small and quiet or grand. They feel and promote interconnectedness and endeavor to be aware of materials, resources, and channels of communication. Sacred nourishes itself by retreating, and takes great solace in privacy and solitude, ritual, and unbounded time. Sacred tends to be singularly focused and intensely devoted to personal values or causes. On a dark day, they can be righteous and critical. With spiritual communion as their core inspiration, Sacred is built to live in service to the whole and longs to do so through their own creative outlets.

**LOOK & FEEL:** Aesthetic is based on more on feelings and stories than literal fashion—anything goes if it is deemed cherished. Asian and Eastern influences; attracted to heritages of many cultures. Lean toward simplistic or graceful design. Try to engage sensuality in all matters: lighting, lyrics, rhythms, scent; warmth, quality fabrics, pure colors, pleasurable tastes.

*adored, adviser, affirming, angelic, blessed, cherished, consecrated, creativity, dear, divine, enduring, evolving, full of life, hallowed, holy, important, ministerial, mystic, natural, organic, peaceful, positive, pure, quiet, religious, resourceful, revered, rewarded, resurrected, sacramental, sacrosanct, sanctified, sent from above, solemn, spiritual, sublime, supernatural, transcendent*

## Sensual / Sensuality / Sensuous

**SPIRIT:** Sensual eats life whole. They wrote the book on the pleasure principle. For Sensual, physical and erotic comfort and aesthetic delight are akin to spiritual fulfillment. Even more than their love for the arts—both mystical and material—cuisine, erotica, and/nature, it is Sensuals intuitive capacities that are so defining. Sensual is not only a loyal devotee of the five earthly senses but are gifted with extrasensory capacities such as intuition, a keen awareness of timing, and psychic sensitivity. Their shadow side can be predatorily seductive or will tend to over-spiritualize in an effort to justify. Holistically inclined, Sensual dances with the terra firma and the cosmos. They can be, surprisingly to some, very practical, commonsensical, and clearheaded, identifying as closely with their minds and intellectual curiosity as their physical nature and appetites.

**LOOK & FEEL:** Sexy, erotic; either highly feminine or strongly masculine. Lush, generous, flowing, supple, curvy. Tactile. Vibrant colors. Plethora of sights and smells and sounds. Cosmopolitan cooking. Mystical, ethereal. Healing.

*arousing, atmosphere, aura, awareness, bodily, clearheaded, clever, common consciousness, delightful, discernment, dreamy, epicurean, erotic, exciting, feeling, fleshly, hot, imaginative, insightful, intellect, intuition, loving, lush, luxury, perception, pleasure, premonition, reasoning, recreation, rejoicing, relaxation, self-indulgent, sensitive, sentiment, sexy, smart, soul, spirit, sultry, tactile, wise*

## Simple / Simplified / Simplistic / Simply

**SPIRIT:** Simply is authentic and unpretentious. No-nonsense and never one for airs or embellishment, they are typically humble and modest. What you see is what you get. Simply loathes excessiveness, waste, and clutter—both materially and psychologically. Deception and personal politics irritate them on the deepest level. What's unnecessary is disheartening. Simply is a direct communicator. They express themselves clearly and candidly. They love to find out the story behind the story, get their point across, and be heard, and they won't back down from an argument. In fact, they can be incredibly persistent and stubborn, to the point of becoming entrenched. For better or for worse, they're great at cutting corners. Simply loves to find the most logical or ideal solutions   utility and purposefulness are at the top of their list. They are remarkably durable and hearty spirits. Simply has a keen way of knowing what's most important or essential in every dimension and deeply relishes the basic necessities and pleasures of life.

**LOOK & FEEL:** Clean, pared down, balanced. Basic, organic. Fundamental. Austere, plain. Open spaces. Well organized. Tidy. Can range from ultramodern and stark to sheer elegance. Never ostentatious or showy.

*clear, common, clarity, classical, direct, ease, elemental, honest, humble, innocent, integrity, intelligible, modest, natural, open, primitive, pure, quiet, restrained, sincere, straightforward, unity*

## Sophisticated / Sophistication

**SPIRIT:** Sophisticated is a knowledge hunter. High-minded and thoughtful, they are perpetually seeking life education, either through world travel or on-the-road adventures, schooling, and training. They are particularly fond of the visual and dramatic arts and are voracious and usually eclectic readers. They are keen to know the meaning of things. They notice nuances and trace through lines; they can simplify an epic and see grandness in simplicity. Sophisticated is truly interested. They ask penetrating questions and will keep on asking. Their central relationships are intense, and they tend to have a mosaic of associations   quirky, nurturing, eccentric, and wise. You can't fool a Sophisticated; they are anything but naive, though they won't necessarily wear their perceptions on their sleeves. Their psyches and personas are multilayered, and thus Sophisticated may be difficult to get close to or may appear to be above it all. They have refined internal systems for making decisions—they think things through in their own way, in their own time.

**LOOK & FEEL:** Classic, refined; collected from various cultures or places around the world. Ornate, sumptuous. Well-made and engineered. Thoughtful. Top quality. Complex but elegant. High integrity.

*adult, citified, classic, cool, cosmopolitan, cultivated, cultured, elaborate, elegant, experienced, hip, intricate, involved, jet set, knowing, mature, modern, multifaceted, practical, refined, schooled, seasoned, sharp, smooth, streetwise, studied, subtle, uptown, worldly-wise*

## Structured

**SPIRIT:** Structured stands for reason and integrity. They build things: systems, structures, achievements. They will map things out and gather all of the essential resources— emotional and material—before they jump into a new endeavor. They don't like to rush, and they are not prone to shortcuts. They have a gift for recognizing and analyzing patterns, code, and themes in situations, artistic works, and group dynamics. They love to engineer and affect change; that's why they get up every morning. They firmly believe that you need to know the old-fashioned and traditional ways of doing things in order to be on the leading edge. Structured is gratified to be master of a few things, rather than jacks-of-all-trades. They take pride in what they do. Without enough rest and playfulness in their lives, Structured can become overly analytical and disconnected from its heart. Structured is very much in touch with its own foundation—fundamentals, values, guiding beliefs—and is rarely swayed from its ideals.

**LOOK & FEEL:** Carefully built, sturdy, solid, heavy, graphic, bold. Attention to detail, well-engineered. Ordered, tidy. Rooted in history. Original, primitive.

*basic, business-like, careful, constitutional, deliberate, disciplined, efficient, elemental, exact, fixed, framed, grass roots, logical, methodical, meticulous,*

*painstaking, planned, precise, radical,*
*supportive, systematic, theoretical,*
*together, vital*

## Tailored

**SPIRIT:** Tailored thrives on creating environments, systems, and situations. Always improving and enhancing, Tailored loves to make old things better and to create new things from nothing. They appreciate formality and appropriateness; being proper and traditional comes naturally. Tailored in excess is overly routinized or controlling, which can lead to worry. Tailored simplify and pare down conversations, decor, and schedules. They are thoughtful and considerate, taking into account everyone's needs and the situation at hand. Tailored is happy to be in a support role, and with their innate ability to create structure can devise amazing plans and strategies for others to follow. At their best, Tailored balances a desire for structure and simplicity, with a flowing, creative outlet.

**LOOK & FEEL:** Simple, trim, or severe in line or design; neat, classic, crafted, crisp, custom-built, custom-fit, custom-made.

*classic, constructive, controlled, customized, designer, detailed, devoted, exclusive, formatted, genuine, innovative, made to measure, made to order, organized, optimized, perfectly fitted, precise, regimented, refined, ritual, simplified, simplistic, solution-oriented, strategic, systematized, thorough, thoughtful, tradition, quality*

## Timeless

**SPIRIT:** Timeless is deeply interested in philosophies, ideas, customs, stories, and objects that have stood the test of time. They pride themselves on their loyalty and staying power and seek to endure with grace. Somewhat sentimental, they choose their quality and avoid trendiness and gimmicks; they would rather have a few quality relationships or possessions than numerous less-than-amazing friendships or things. With a long-term focus, Timeless is willing to delay gratification and choose not to rush. When stressed or strained, they will react in one of two ways: either clinging to structure and regimen, or waffling and flaking out. Independent spirits but inclusive and community-oriented thinkers, they consider who and what has come before and what is being created for the future. Their motto is Quality + Endurance = Luxuriousness.

**LOOK & FEEL:** Sophisticated, classic, traditional, elegant; polished, clean lines; from crisp and tailored to graceful, fluid, and comfortable; ranges from Old World to contemporary design. Solid, quality; durable or very refined textiles. Never goes out of style.

*abiding, ageless, always, ceaseless, classic, connected, constant, continual, dateless, enduring, everlasting, lasting, perennial, permanent, perpetual, persisting, prevailing, refined, relentless, steady, sustaining, unbroken, unchanging, wear on, wear well*

## Traditional

**SPIRIT:** Traditional gets tremendous joy from nourishing a sense of community and family, whether within a neighborhood, group, organization, or among family members and friends. They are curious and learn from what has come before, especially anything pertaining to time-honored orthodox doctrines and practices. Traditional is keenly interested in finding the best way to do something. What has worked in the past? and What will work now and in the future? are their guiding questions. And when they find something that works, they happily dispense advice, and share best finds, how-tos, and personal learning. If they can't find an established way of doing something that works for them, Traditional will create their own customs, routines, or rituals and ultimately legacies. They build things to last—relationships, creative works, a sense of home and place, policies, products—and they hang in there. Traditional typically has a strong personal sense of right and wrong, which at times can cause rigidity. At their best, Traditional is actively curious about the perspectives and creations of other cultures.

**LOOK & FEEL:** Feminine/womanly for women. Masculine/manly for men. Respectful, classic, timeless, enduring, conventional.

*accustomed, acknowledged, ancestral, classic, classical, conventional, custom-*

*ary, doctrinal, established, family, folk, historic, homespun, handmade, heritage, legacy, native, natural, old, oral, origins, passed on, popular, rooted, time-honored, timeless*

## Understated

**SPIRIT:** Understated coined the phrase *less is more.* Their strength is founded on simplicity and grace. With a tremendous sense of decorum and appropriateness, Understated suits up, shows up, and rises to the occasion. Subtle, patient, and refined, Understated knows that actions speak louder than words. At their best, Understated trusts that things will work themselves out if they simply allow them to. Artfully diplomatic with a gentle touch, they compose their inner circle with those who are able to understand and appreciate their sensitive nature, yet Understated is not fragile—to the contrary. They have a deep undercurrent of ideals and values by which they navigate. Zealousness, the hard sell, and aggression sends Understated in an about-face. Their challenge is not to take things personally and to rest assured in their own values and good judgment. Understated is content to work behind the scenes as supportive forces or masterminds, happy to make others look good. Of course, they believe that just a little bit of glamour or nonchalance goes a long way, and it is precisely that kind of restrained elegance that is their most attractive and empowering quality.

**LOOK & FEEL:** Classic, elegant, refined, modest. Comfortable, cushy, smooth. Diffused, hazy, muted, misty, pale, pastel, shaded. Harmonious, symmetrical, well-proportioned, streamlined. Quiet, tranquil, melodious.

*delicate, caressing, easygoing, laid-back, light, loose, low-key, mellow, mild, played down, quiet, relaxed, restful, softened, soothing, subdued, subtle, sweet, temperate, toned down, twilight, whispered*

# Creative Edge Words...
## a starter of possibilities

Following is a list of 20% words to inspire you. Be sure to refer to both a dictionary and a thesaurus when reviewing these words. We highly recommend dictionary.com. This list is by no means exhaustive. Keep looking if you don't feel the "click" with one of these words.

adventure / adventurous

affinity

allure / alluring

appreciation / appreciated

artistic / art / artful

avant-garde

balance / balanced

basic

beautiful / beauty

bohemian

bold / boldly

brilliance / brilliant

Buddhist

calm

casual

celebrated / celebration

character

charm / charming

cherish / cherished / cherishes / cherishing

chic

choice

classic / classical

collection

colorful / color

comfort / comfortable / comforting

composed

connected / connection

constructed / constructive

contemporary

contribution

cosmopolitan

couture

cozy

craft / crafted / craftmanship

creative / creativity

cultivated / cultivation

cultured / culture / cultural

current

custom / customized

dancer / dancing

daring

darling

dazzle / dazzling

dear

decadence / decadent

decorative

dedicated / dedication

defined / defining

delicate

delight / delightful

deluxe

demure

deep / depth

design / designed / designing / designs

devoted / devotional

dignified / dignity

discovery

distinct / distinction

dramatic

dynamic

earth / earthly

ease

east / eastern

eccentric

edge / edgy

elegance / elegant

elemental / elements

empowered / empowering

enchanting / enchantment

endearing

enduring

energetic / energy

era

esprit

essence / essential

exotic

expressed / expression / expressive

extravagance / extravagant

faith / faithful

fanciful / fancy

fantasy

feminine / femininity

festive / festivity

flair

flamboyance / flamboyant

flirt / flirtatious / flirty

flourish / flourishing

fluid / fluidity

focused

free-spirited

fresh

friend / friendship

fulfilled / fulfillment

fun

fusion

futuristic / future

generosity / generous

genteel / gentility

gentleman

genuine

gift / gifted

glow / glowed / glowing

goddess

grace / graceful / gracious

grand / grandeur

harmony / harmonious

heart / hearted

heritage

hip

hippy

home / homespun

honest / honesty

hope / hopeful

ideal / idealist

independent / indie

industrial / industrious

innovative / innovation

inspiration / inspired / inspiring

instinct / instinctive

integrity

intellectual

intention / intentional

international

intuition / intuitive

invitation / inviting

lady

lasting

lavish

legacy

legend / legendary

light

love / lovely

luminosity / luminous

lush

lustre / lustrous

luxe / luxury

magic / magical

majestic

man / manly

masculine

material

maverick

meaning / meaningful

memories

metropolitan

minimalism / minimalist

modern / modernist

modest / modesty

mysterious / mystery / mystique / mystical

native

natural / nature

new / nouveau

nobility / noble

nostalgia / nostalgic

opulence / opulent

organic

original

ornate

passion / passionate

peace / peaceful

peasant

performance / performer

philosophical

pioneer

play / playful / playing

poem / poet / poetic

popular

posh

power / powerful

precious

presence

present

pretty

punk

pure / purely / purity

quaint

quality

quiet

radiance / radiant

rare / rarity

reality / realized

rebel / rebellious

refined / refining

reflection / reflective

remarkable

respect / respectful

resonance

revolutionary

rich / riches / richness

romance / romantic

rugged

rustic

sacred

select / selection / selective

sensibility / sensible

sense / sensual / sensuality / sensuous

sentiment / sentimental

serene / serenity

sexuality / sexy

shimmer / shimmering

signature

simple / simplified / simplistic / simply

sincere / sincerity

soft / softness

solid / solidity

sophisticate / sophisticated / sophistication

soul / soulful

space / spacious

sparkle / sparkling

special / specialness

spirit / spiritual

story

strength / strong

structured / structural

style / stylish

subtle

sultry

sumptuous

surprise / surprising

sweet

tailored

theater / theatrical

thoughtful

timeless

tradition / traditional

traveler

treasure

tribal

truth / truthful

unique / uniqueness

valuable / valued

vibrance / vibrancy

vintage

vital / vitality

vivid

vixen

vogue

success / successful

warm

western

whimsical / whimsy

wild

woman / womanly

wonder / wonderful

worth / worthy

value / valued

vision / visionary

zen

# Ask-a-Friend Survey

Oh would some power the gift give us,
to see ourselves as others see us!

—ROBERT BURNS

Some caring objectivity could prove useful as
you define your Style Statement. Photocopy
this page and ask a good friend or partner to
show you yourself through their eyes.

HOW WOULD YOU DESCRIBE MY FASHION STYLE?

WHAT DO YOU THINK IS MY GREATEST PERSONAL STRENGTH?

WHAT DO YOU THINK IT WOULD DO ME GOOD TO LET GO OF IN MY WARDROBE, MY HOME, OR MY PSYCHE?

WHEN DO YOU FEEL THAT I AM AT MY BEST?

WHAT DO YOU WISH I WAS LESS OF, FOR MY SAKE?

WHEN HAVE YOU SEEN ME LOOKING MY MOST FABULOUS?

WHAT DO YOU THINK I COULD GIVE MYSELF MORE CREDIT FOR OR CELEBRATE MORE?

# Gratitude

We each feel incredibly blessed to be married to men who are bright, strong-willed, and life-loving. Cameron Thorn and Scott Johnson: protective, comforting, above-and-beyond supportive, and sexy. Most simply and truly put, we could not have done this without them.

If you're really lucky, at some point in your life you will receive a resounding *yes!* that affirms your life calling and flings the future wide open. In our case, that came from Tina Bennett, our literary agent: gracious, indomitable, and deeply wise. When we grow up, we want to be just like her. Svetlana Katz became our much-relied-on wing woman on this adventure. We navigated by her pragmatism and good judgment—all delivered with loving care. Malcolm Gladwell had the good sense to find us charming enough to provide us with a life-changing introduction. Michelle Pante's acumen, tenacity, and rock-solid support kept our spirits up and our vision clear. It has been an honor to earn her loyalty.

Photographer Gregory Crow not only delivered what we hoped for, but became a true friend in the process. Gary Tooth of Empire Design became jeweler to our words and images. With skill and understanding, he set them into something more beautiful than we'd imagined.

Each of the individuals profiled in this book has a special place in our hearts. Every one of them is a star. Heather Kennedy coordinated hundreds of requests—on deadline. We will be forever grateful. Grace Kerina ennobles our work with her good sense and love.

It is a privilege to be supported by such a distinguished publisher as Little, Brown and Company. Terry Adams, Marlena Bittner, Judy Clain, Sophie Cottrell, Heather Fain, Keith Hayes, Michael Pietsch, Marie Salter, Tracy Williams, Andrea Vazzano, and a league of others make for a first-class team.

Many people supported our creative process in many different ways: Howard Airey, Leslie Alexander, Andrew Atkins, Michael Barden, Eileen Baumgartner, Kathleen Beaumont, Billie, Melody Biringer, Gregg Brown, Belinda Bruce, Cathy Byers, Amy Childs, Martha Carter, Kim Christie, Camilla Coates, Judythe Cohen, Malcolm Collings, Lyn Connock, Desiree Daniel, Catherine Diamond, Stefan Doering, Patsy Duggan, Sara Gori, Mary Gowans, Uli Hobruecker, Candis and Timothy Hoey, Kelly Hoey, Dolly Hopkins, Kip Horton, Paul Jervis, Eric Johnson, Judy Johnson, Peter and Cathy Johnson, Navjit Kandola, Robert Kent, Tamara Komuniecki, Sherri Koop, Sophie Lambert, Ladies Who Launch, Dennis and Kitty LaPorte, Peter Laprés, Patricia Larsen, John Lau, Theresa Lenardon, Sarah LeRoy, Jonathon Lo, Colette Matter, Sheila Martineau, Tammy Mazak, Patricia McCarthy, Robert McCarthy, Skippy McCarthy, Brenda McAllister, Ward McAllister, Annabelle McCorquodale, Donald McMillan, Laura Mountjoy, Tschitschi Mundhenk, Kirk Oliver, Joshua Pettinato, Robert Quigg, Lee-Anne Ragan, Karryn Ransom, Steve Rechtschaffner, Shannon Read, Glenda Reid, Dorothea Roberts, Bridget Ross, Renée Rouleau, Rikia Saddy, Kate Schafer, Jennifer Seymour, Tanya Schroenroth, Leila and Matt Shaw, Ravi Sidhoo, Christina Song, John Thompson, Keri Thorn, Kathy Turcic, Donna and Brad VanEvery, Leisa Washington, Nancy White, Peter White, Fred Yada, Jamie York, Carol Zhong, and special thanks to Stinky Zimmermanc.

Harper LaPorte Johnson is pure inspiration. And our sisters—by blood and by love—are the closest women in our lives, who make us laugh at ourselves, remind us who we are, and keep us real. And if they are proud of us, we can be proud of ourselves.

# Behind the Scenes

CREATIVE TEAM

**GREGORY CROW, PHOTOGRAPHER**

Originally from New Zealand, Gregory has become an established and recognized photographer in Canada over the last decade. Working across the globe, his signature minimal clean lines and timeless images have earned him industry accolades and awards.

gregorycrow.com

**BRENNDAN LAIRD, PHOTOGRAPHY ASSISTANT**

A fashion and landscape photographer, Brenndan has a degree in photography from the Emily Carr Institute of Art and Design.

brenndanlaird.com

**SEAN FRITH, PHOTOGRAPHY ASSISTANT**

seanfrith.com

**GARY TOOTH/EMPIRE DESIGN STUDIO, GRAPHIC DESIGNER**

Empire Design Studio creates unique and engaging graphic solutions for a variety of media. The Studio applies creative thinking across the communications spectrum, from print and publishing design to comprehensive branding strategies. In addition, it is the Studio's mission to employ environmentally responsible, sustainable, and socially beneficial practices throughout its creative process.

empiredesignstudio.com

**MELANIE NEUFELD, LEAD MAKEUP ARTIST**

A freelance and MAC makeup artist for eleven years, Melanie is represented by the Liz Bell Agency in Vancouver.

**KATINA TROTZUK**

Katina was the makeup artist for the Style Statement profiles of Audrey Beaulac, Patsy Duggan, Dorothea Roberts, and Victoria Roberts.

**WEYLON**

Weylon was the makeup artist for the Style Statement profiles of Candis Hoey, Klee Larsen, and Joan Pham.

We are grateful for the generous loans of clothing and space from the following vendors: Jacqueline Conoir, JC Studio, Vancouver (dress for Carrie McCarthy's Style Statement profile); City Cigar, Vancouver (location for Donald McMillan); Inform Interiors, Vancouver (location for Audrey Beaulac and Andrew Williamson and Kate Stevenson); East is East Restaurant, Vancouver (location for Navjit Kandola); Queensborough Boxing Club, New Westminster, BC (location for Joan Pham); Banana Republic, Vancouver (suit for Andrew Williamson); Museum of Anthropology, Vancouver (location for Lyn Connock); Jack's Used Building Materials, Burnaby, BC (location for Klee Larsen); and Bernstein & Gold, Vancouver (linens for Melody Biringer). We also acknowledge the support of Gravity Pope Shoes in Vancouver; the divine skills of Candis Hoey of Studio C, Victoria, BC; and Zoë Broomsgrove of Zoho's Style & Dreadlock Shop, Vancouver.

Visit **www.carrieanddanielle.com**, for:

- **IDEAS & ICONS**, OUR DAILY E-MAGAZINE.

- MORE INQUIRY QUESTIONS.

- AN EXTENDED AND ALWAYS EVOLVING VERSION OF THE STYLE VOCABULARY.

- INSPIRATIONAL QUOTES.

- A DOWNLOADABLE STYLE STATEMENT JOURNAL.

- A DOWNLOADABLE STYLE STATEMENT GROUP GUIDE AND COUPLE'S GUIDE.

- AND PLENTY OF INSPIRING AND BEAUTIFUL THINGS TO SUPPORT YOU TO COMMUNICATE WHO YOU ARE IN ALL YOU DO.